A Biography of Edmund Spenser

John W. Hales

Contents

A BIOGRAPHY OF
EDMUND SPENSER

BY

John W. Hales

EDMUND SPENSER.

Ille velut fidis arcana sodalibus olim
Credebat libris; neque, si male cesserat, unquam
Decurrens alio, neque si bene; quo fit ut omnis
Votiva pateat veluti descripta tabella
Vita senis.

Hither, as to their fountain, other stars
Repairing in their urns draw golden light.

The life of Spenser is wrapt in a similar obscurity to

that which hides from us his great predecessor Chaucer, and his still greater contemporary Shakspere. As in the case of Chaucer, our principal external authorities are a few meagre entries in certain official documents, and such facts as may be gathered from his works. The birth-year of each poet is determined by inference. The circumstances in which each died are a matter of controversy. What sure information we have of the intervening events of the life of each one is scanty and interrupted. So far as our knowledge goes, it shows some slight positive resemblance between their lives. They were both connected with the highest society of their times; both enjoyed court favour, and enjoyed it in the substantial shape of pensions. They were both men of remarkable learning. They were both natives of London. They both died in the close vicinity of Westminster Abbey, and lie buried near each other in that splendid cemetery. Their geniuses were eminently different: that of Chaucer was the active type, Spenser's of the contemplative; Chaucer was dramatic, Spenser philosophical; Chaucer objective, Spenser subjective; but in the external circumstances, so far as we know them, amidst which these great poets moved, and in the mist which for the most part enfolds those circumstances, there is considerable likeness.

Spenser is frequently alluded to by his contemporaries; they most ardently recognised in him, as we shall see, a great poet, and one that might justly be associated with the one supreme poet whom this country had then produced--with Chaucer, and they paid him constant tributes of respect and admiration; but these mentions of him do not generally supply any biographical details.

The earliest notice of him that may in any sense
be termed biographical occurs in a sort of handbook to
the monuments of Westminster Abbey, published by Camden
in 1606. Amongst the 'Reges, Regin{ae}, Nobiles, et alij
in Ecclesia Collegiata B. Petri Westmonasterii sepulti
usque ad annum 1606' is enrolled the name of Spenser,
with the following brief obituary:

'Edmundus Spencer Londinensis, Anglicorum Poetarum
nostri seculi facile princeps, quod ejus poemata
faventibus Musis et victuro genio conscripta
comprobant. Obijt immatura morte anno salutis 1598, et
prope Galfredum Chaucerum conditur qui felicissime
po{e"}sin Anglicis literis primus illustravit. In quem
h{ae}c scripta sunt epitaphia:--

> Hic prope Chaucerum situs est Spenserius, illi
>   Proximus ingenio proximus ut tumulo.

> Hic prope Chaucerum, Spensere poeta, poetam
>   Conderis, et versu quam tumulo propior.
> Anglica, te vivo, vixit plausitque po{e"}sis;
>   Nunc moritura timet, te moriente, mori.'

'Edmund Spencer of London, far the first of the
English Poets of our age, as his poems prove, written
under the smile of the Muses, and with a genius
destined to live. He died prematurely in the year of
salvation 1598, and is buried near Geoffrey Chaucer,
who was the first most happily to set forth poetry in
English writing: and on him were written these
epitaphs:--

> Here nigh to Chaucer Spenser lies; to whom

In genius next he was, as now in tomb.

Here nigh to Chaucer, Spenser, stands thy
hearse,{1}
Still nearer standst thou to him in thy verse.
Whilst thou didst live, lived English poetry;
Now thou art dead, it fears that it shall die.'

The next notice is found in Drummond's account of
Ben Jonson's conversations with him in the year 1618:
'Spencer's stanzas pleased him not, nor his
matter. The meaning of the allegory of his Fairy Queen
he had delivered in writing to Sir Walter Rawleigh,
which was, "that by the Bleating Beast he understood
the Puritans, and by the false Duessa the Queen of
Scots." He told, that Spencer's goods were robbed by
the Irish, and his house and a little child burnt, he
and his wife escaped, and after died for want of bread
in King Street; he refused 20 pieces sent to him by my
lord Essex, and said he was sure he had no time to
spend them.'{2}
The third record occurs in Camden's History of
Queen Elizabeth (Annales rerum Anglicarum et
Hibernicarum regnante Elizabetha), first published in
a complete form in 1628. There the famous antiquary
registering what demises marked the year 1598 (our
March 25, 1598, to March 24, 1599), adds to his list
Edmund Spenser, and thus writes of him: 'Ed. Spenserus,
patria Londinensis, Cantabrigienis autem alumnus, Musis
adeo arridentibus natus ut omnes Anglicos superioris
{ae}vi Poetas, ne Chaucero quidem concive excepto,
superaret. Sed peculiari Poetis fato semper cum
paupertate conflictatus, etsi Greio Hiberni{ae} proregi

fuerit ab epistolis. Vix enim ibi secessum et
scribendi otium nactus, quam a rebellibus {e\} laribus
ejectus et bonis spoliatus, in Angliam inops reversus
statim exspiravit, Westmonasterii prope Chaucerum
impensis comitis Essexi{ae} inhumatus, Po{e"}tis funus
ducentibus flebilibusque carminibus et calamis in
tumulum conjectis.'{3} This is to say: 'Edmund
Spenser, a Londoner by birth, and a scholar also of the
University of Cambridge, born under so favourable an
aspect of the Muses that he surpassed all the English
Poets of former times, not excepting Chaucer himself,
his fellow-citizen. But by a fate which still follows
Poets, he always wrestled with poverty, though he had
been secretary to the Lord Grey, Lord Deputy of
Ireland. For scarce had he there settled himself into
a retired privacy and got leisure to write, when he was
by the rebels thrown out of his dwelling, plundered of
his goods, and returned to England a poor man, where he
shortly after died and was interred at Westminster,
near to Chaucer, at the charge of the Earl of Essex,
his hearse being attended by poets, and mournful
elegies and poems with the pens that wrote them thrown
into his tomb.'{4}

In 1633, Sir James Ware prefaced his edition of
Spenser's prose work on the State of Ireland with these
remarks:--

'How far these collections may conduce to the
knowledge of the antiquities and state of this land,
let the fit reader judge: yet something I may not passe
by touching Mr. Edmund Spenser and the worke it selfe,
lest I should seem to offer injury to his worth, by
others so much celebrated. Hee was borne in London of
an ancient and noble family, and brought up in the

Universitie of Cambridge, where (as the fruites of his
after labours doe manifest) he mispent not his time.
After this he became secretary to Arthur Lord Grey of
Wilton, Lord Deputy of Ireland, a valiant and worthy
governour, and shortly after, for his services to the
Crowne, he had bestowed upon him by Queene Elizabeth,
3,000 acres of land in the countie of Corke. There he
finished the latter part of that excellent poem of his
"Faery Queene," which was soone after unfortunately
lost by the disorder and abuse of his servant, whom he
had sent before him into England, being then a
rebellibus (as Camden's words are) {e\} laribus ejectus
et bonis spoliatus. He deceased at Westminster in the
year 1599 (others have it wrongly 1598), soon after his
return into England, and was buried according to his
own desire in the collegiat church there, neere unto
Chaucer whom he worthily imitated (at the costes of
Robert Earle of Essex), whereupon this epitaph was
framed.' And then are quoted the epigrams already
given from Camden.

The next passage that can be called an account of
Spenser is found in Fuller's **Worthies of England**,
first published in 1662, and runs as follows:--

'Edmond Spencer, born in this city (London), was
brought up in Pembroke-hall in Cambridge, where he
became an excellent scholar; but especially most happy
in English Poetry; as his works do declare, in which
the many Chaucerisms used (for I will not say affected
by him) are thought by the ignorant to be blemishes,
known by the learned to be beauties, to his book; which
notwithstanding had been more saleable, if more
conformed to our modern language.

'There passeth a story commonly told and believed,

that Spencer presenting his poems to queen Elizabeth, she, highly affected therewith, commanded the lord Cecil, her treasurer, to give him an hundred pound; and when the treasurer (a good steward of the queen's money) alledged that the sum was too much; "Then give him," quoth the queen, "What is reason;" to which the lord consented, but was so busied, belike, about matters of higher concernment, that Spencer received no reward, whereupon he presented this petition in a small piece of paper to the queen in her progress:--

> I was promis'd on a time,
> To have reason for my rhyme;
> From that time unto this season,
> I receiv'd nor rhyme nor reason.

'Hereupon the queen gave strict order (not without some check to her treasurer), for the present payment of the hundred pounds the first intended unto him.

'He afterwards went over into Ireland, secretary to the lord Gray, lord deputy thereof; and though that his office under his lord was lucrative, yet he got no estate; but saith my author "peculiari poetis fato semper cum paupertate conflictatus est." So that it fared little better with him than with William Xilander the German (a most excellent linguist, antiquary, philosopher and mathematician), who was so poor, that (as Thuanus saith), he was thought "fami non famae scribere."

'Returning into England, he was robb'd by the rebels of what little he had; and dying for grief in great want, anno 1598, was honourably buried nigh Chaucer in Westminster, where this distich concludeth his epitaph on his monument

> Anglica, te vivo, vixit plausitque poesis;
>   Nunc moritura timet, te moriente, mori.'

> Whilst thou didst live, liv'd English poetry
> Which fears now thou art dead, that she shall die.

'Nor must we forget, that the expence of his funeral and monument was defrayed at the sole charge of Robert, first of that name, earl of Essex.'

The next account is given by Edward Phillips in his Theatrum Po{e"}tarum Anglicanorum, first published in 1675. This Phillips was, as is well known, Milton's nephew, and according to Warton, in his edition of Milton's juvenile poems, 'there is good reason to suppose that Milton threw many additions and corrections into the Theatrum Po{e"}tarum.' Phillips' words therefore have an additional interest for us. 'Edmund Spenser,' he writes, 'the first of our English poets that brought heroic poesy to any perfection, his "Fairy Queen" being for great invention and poetic heighth, judg'd little inferior, if not equal to the chief of the ancient Greeks and Latins, or modern Italians; but the first poem that brought him into esteem was his "Shepherd's Calendar," which so endeared him to that noble patron of all vertue and learning Sir Philip Sydney, that he made him known to Queen Elizabeth, and by that means got him preferred to be secretary to his brother{5} Sir Henry Sidney, who was sent deputy into Ireland, where he is said to have written his "Faerie Queen;" but upon the return of Sir

Henry, his employment ceasing, he also return'd into England, and having lost his great friend Sir Philip, fell into poverty, yet made his last refuge to the Queen's bounty, and had 500*l.* ordered him for his support, which nevertheless was abridged to 100*l.* by Cecil, who, hearing of it, and owing him a grudge for some reflections in Mother Hubbard's Tale, cry'd out to the queen, What! all this for a song? This he is said to have taken so much to heart, that he contracted a deep melancholy, which soon after brought his life to a period. So apt is an ingenuous spirit to resent a slighting, even from the greatest persons; thus much I must needs say of the merit of so great a poet from so great a monarch, that as it is incident to the best of poets sometimes to flatter some royal or noble patron, never did any do it more to the height, or with greater art or elegance, if the highest of praises attributed to so heroic a princess can justly be termed flattery.'{6}

When Spenser's works were reprinted--the first three books of the **Faerie Queene** for the seventh time--in 1679, there was added an account of his life. In 1687, Winstanley, in his Lives of the most famous English Poets, wrote a formal biography.

These are the oldest accounts of Spenser that have been handed down to us. In several of them mythical features and blunders are clearly discernible. Since Winstanley's time, it may be added, Hughes in 1715, Dr. Birch in 1731, Church in 1758, Upton in that same year, Todd in 1805, Aikin in 1806, Robinson in 1825, Mitford in 1839, Prof. Craik in 1845, Prof. Child in 1855, Mr. Collier in 1862, Dr. Grosart in 1884, have re-told what little there is to tell, with various additions and subtractions.

Our external sources of information are, then, extremely scanty. Fortunately our internal sources are somewhat less meagre. No poet ever more emphatically lived in his poetry than did Spenser. The Muses were, so to speak, his own bosom friends, to whom he opened all his heart. With them he conversed perpetually on the various events of his life; into their ears he poured forth constantly the tale of his joys and his sorrows, of his hopes, his fears, his distresses.

He was not one of those poets who can put off themselves in their works, who can forego their own interests and passions, and live for the time an extraneous life. There is an intense personality about all his writings, as in those of Milton and of Wordsworth. In reading them you can never forget the poet in the poem. They directly and fully reflect the poet's own nature and his circumstances. They are, as it were, fine spiritual diaries, refined self-portraitures. Horace's description of his own famous fore-runner, quoted at the head of this memoir, applies excellently to Spenser. On this account the scantiness of our external means of knowing Spenser is perhaps the less to be regretted. Of him it is eminently true that we may know him from his works. His poems are his best biography. In the sketch of his life to be given here his poems shall be our one great authority.

Notes

{1} Compare 'Underneath this sable *hearse*, &c.'
{2} Works of William Drummond of Hawthornden. Edinburgh, 1711, p. 225.
{3} *Annales*, ed. *Hearne*, iii. 783.
{4} *History of Elizabeth, Queen of England.* Ed. 1688, pp. 564, 565.
{5} Father
{6} *Theatrum Poet. Anglic.*, ed. Brydges, 1800, pp. 148, 149.

CHAPTER I.

1552-1579.

FROM SPENSER'S BIRTH TO THE PUBLICATION OF THE SHEPHEARD'S CALENDAR.

Edmund Spenser was born in London in the year 1552, or possibly 1551. For both these statements we have directly or indirectly his own authority. In his *Prothalamion* he sings of certain swans whom in a vision he saw floating down the river 'Themmes,' that

> At length they all to mery London came,
> To mery London, my most kyndly nurse,
> That to me gave this lifes first native sourse,
> Though from another place I take my name,
> An house of auncient fame.

A MS. note by Oldys the antiquary in Winstanley's *Lives of the most famous English Poets*, states that the precise locality of his birth was East Smithfield. East Smithfield lies just to the east of the Tower, and in the middle of the sixteenth century, when the Tower was still one of the chief centres of London life and importance, was of course a neighbourhood of far different rank and degree from its present social status. The date of his birth is concluded with sufficient certainty from one of his sonnets, viz. sonnet 60; which it is pretty well ascertained was composed in the year 1593. These sonnets are, as well shall see, of the amorous wooing sort; in the one of them just mentioned, the sighing poet declares that it is but a year since he fell in love, but that the year has seemed to him longer

> Then al those fourty which my life out-went.

Hence it is gathered that he was most probably born in 1552. The inscription, then, over his tomb in Westminster Abbey errs in assigning his birth to 1553; though the error is less flagrant than that perpetrated by the inscription that preceded the present one, which set down as his natal year 1510.

Of his parents the only fact secured is that his
mother's name was Elizabeth. This appears from sonnet
74, where he apostrophizes those

Most happy letters! fram'd by skilfull trade
With which that happy name was first desynd,
The which three times thrise happy hath me made,
With guifts of body, fortune and of mind.
The first my being to me gave by kind
From mothers womb deriv'd by dew descent.

The second is the Queen, the third 'my love, my lives
last ornament.' A careful examination by Mr. Collier
and others of what parish registers there are extant in
such old churches as stand near East Smithfield--the
Great Fire, it will be remembered, broke out some
distance west of the Tower, and raged mainly westward--
has failed to discover any trace of the infant Spenser
or his parents. An 'Edmund Spenser' who is mentioned
in the Books of the Treasurer of the Queen's Chamber in
1569, as paid for bearing letters from Sir Henry
Norris, her Majesty's ambassador in France, to the
Queen,{1} and who with but slight probability has been
surmised to be the poet himself, is scarcely more
plausibly conjectured by Mr. Collier to be the poet's
father. The utter silence about his parents, with the
single exception quoted, in the works of one who, as
has been said above, made poetry the confidante of all
his joys and sorrows, is remarkable.

    Whoever they were, he was well connected on his
father's side at least. 'The nobility of the
Spensers,' writes Gibbon, 'has been illustrated and
enriched by the trophies of Marlborough; but I exhort

them to consider the "Faerie Queen" as the most
precious jewel of their coronet.' Spenser was
connected with the then not ennobled, but highly
influential family of the Spencers of Althorpe,
Northamptonshire. Theirs was the 'house of auncient
fame,' or perhaps we should rather say they too
belonged to the 'house of auncient fame' alluded to in
the quotation made above from the *Prothalamion*. He
dedicates various poems to the daughters of Sir John
Spencer, who was the head of that family during the
poet's youth and earlier manhood down to 1580, and in
other places mentions these ladies with many
expressions of regard and references to his affinity.
'Most faire and vertuous Ladie,' he writes to the
'Ladie Compton and Mountegle,' the fifth daughter, in
his dedication to her of his *Mother Hubberds Tale*,
'having often sought opportunitie by some good meanes
to make knowen to your Ladiship the humble affection
and faithfull duetie, which I have alwaies professed
and am bound to beare to that house, from whence yee
spring, I have at length found occasion to remember the
same by making a simple present to you of these my idle
labours, &c.' To another daughter, 'the right worthy
and vertuous ladie the Ladie Carey,' he dedicates his
Muiopotmos; to another, 'the right honorable the
Ladie Strange,' his *Teares of the Muses*. In the
latter dedication he speaks of 'your particular
bounties, and also some private bands of affinitie,
which it hath pleased your Ladiship to acknowledge.'
It was for this lady Strange, who became subsequently
the wife of Sir Thomas Egerton, that one who came after
Spenser--Milton--wrote the *Arcades*. Of these three
kinswomen, under the names of Phyllis, Charillis, and

sweet Amaryllis, Spenser speaks once more in his Colin
Clouts Come Home Again; he speaks of them as

> The honour of the noble familie
> Of which I meanest boast myself to be.

For the particular branch of the Spencer or Spenser
family--one branch wrote the name with *s*, another
with *c*--to which the poet belonged, it has been well
suggested that it was that settled in East Lancashire
in the neighbourhood of Pendle Forest. It is known on
the authority of his friend Kirke, whom we shall
mention again presently, that Spenser retired to the
North after leaving Cambridge; traces of a Northern
dialect appear in the **Shepheardes Calendar**; the
Christian name Edmund is shown by the parish registers
to have been a favourite with one part of the
Lancashire branch--with that located near Filley Close,
three miles north of Hurstwood, near Burnley.

Spenser then was born in London, probably in East
Smithfield, about a year before those hideous Marian
fires began to blaze in West Smithfield. He had at
least one sister, and probably at least one brother.
His memory would begin to be retentive about the time
of Queen Elizabeth's accession. Of his great
contemporaries, with most of whom he was to be brought
eventually into contact, Raleigh was born at Hayes in
Devonshire in the same year with him, Camden in Old
Bailey in 1551, Hooker near Exeter in or about 1553,
Sidney at Penshurst in 1554, Bacon at York House in the
West Strand, 1561, Shakspere at Stratford-on-Avon in
1564, Robert Devereux, afterwards second earl of Essex,
in 1567.

The next assured fact concerning Spenser is that
he was educated at the Merchant Taylors' School, then
just founded. This we learn from an entry in 'The
Spending of the Money of Robert Nowell, Esq.,' of Reade
Hall, Lancashire, brother of Alexander Nowell, Dean of
St. Paul's. In an accompt of sums 'geven to poor
schollers of dyvers gramare scholles' we find Xs.
given, April 28, 1569, to 'Edmond Spensore Scholler of
the Merchante Tayler Scholl;' and the identification is
established by the occasion being described as 'his
gowinge to Penbrocke Hall in Chambridge,' for we know
that the future poet was admitted a Sizar of Pembroke
College, then styled Hall, Cambridge, in 1569. Thus we
may fairly conclude that Spenser was not only London
born but London bred, though he may have from time to
time sojourned with relatives and connections in
Lancashire{2} before his undergraduateship, as well as
after. Thus a conjecture of Mr. Collier's may
confidently be discarded, who in the muster-book of a
hundred in Warwickshire has noted the record of one
Edmund Spenser as living in 1569 at Kingsbury, and
conjectures that this was the poet's father, and that
perhaps the poet spent his youth in the same county
with Shakspere. It may be much doubted whether it is a
just assumption that every Edmund Spenser that is in
any way or anywhere mentioned in the Elizabethan era
was either the poet or his father. Nor, should it be
allowed that the Spenser of Kingsbury was indeed the
poet's father, could we reasonably indulge in any
pretty picture of a fine friendship between the future
authors of **Hamlet** and of the **Faerie Queene**.
Shakspere was a mere child, not yet passed into the
second of his Seven Ages, when Spenser, being then

about seventeen years old, went up to the University. However, this matter need not be further considered, as there is no evidence whatever to connect Spenser with Warwickshire.

But in picturing to ourselves Spenser's youth we must not think of London as it now is, or of East Smithfield as now cut off from the country by innumerable acres of bricks and mortar. The green fields at that time were not far away from Spenser's birthplace. And thus, not without knowledge and symnpathy, but with appreciative variations, Spenser could re-echo Marot's 'Eglogue au Roy sous les noms de Pan et Robin,' and its descriptions of a boy's rural wanderings and delights. See his Shepheardes Calendar, December:--

> Whilome in youth when flowrd my joyfull spring,
>   Like swallow swift I wandred here and there;
> For heate of heedlesse lust me did so sting,
>   That I oft doubted daunger had no feare:
> I went the wastefull woodes and forrest wide
> Withouten dread of wolves to bene espide.
>
> I wont to raunge amid the mazie thicket
>   And gather nuttes to make my Christmas game,
> And joyed oft to chace the trembling pricket,
>   Or hunt the hartlesse hare till she were tame.
> What wreaked I of wintrie ages waste?
> Tho deemed I my spring would ever last.
>
> How often have I scaled the craggie oke
>   All to dislodge the raven of her nest?
> How have I wearied, with many a stroke,

The stately walnut-tree, the while the rest,
Under the tree fell all for nuttes at strife?
For like to me was libertie and life.

To be sure he is here paraphrasing, and also is writing
in the language of pastoral poetry, that is, the
language of this passage is metaphorical; but it is
equally clear that the writer was intimately and
thoroughly acquainted with that life from which the
metaphors of his original are drawn. He describes a
life he had lived.

It seems probable that he was already an author in
some sort when he went up to Cambridge. In the same
year in which he became an undergraduate there appeared
a work entitled, 'A Theatre wherein be represented as
well the Miseries and Calamities that follow the
Voluptuous Worldlings as also the greate Joyes and
Pleasures which the Faithful do enjoy. An Argument
both Profitable and Delectable to all that sincerely
loue the Word of God. Deuised by S. John Vander
Noodt.' Vander Noodt was a native of Brabant who had
sought refuge in England, 'as well for that I would not
beholde the abominations of the Romyshe Antechrist as
to escape the handes of the bloudthirsty.' 'In the
meane space,' he continues, 'for the avoyding of
idlenesse (the very mother and nourice of all vices) I
have among other my travayles bene occupied aboute thys
little Treatyse, wherein is sette forth the vilenesse
and basenesse of worldely things whiche commonly
withdrawe us from heavenly and spirituall matters.'
This work opens with six pieces in the form of sonnets
styled epigrams, which are in fact identical with the
first six of the ***Visions of Petrarch*** subsequently

published among Spenser's works, in which publication they are said to have been 'formerly translated'. After these so-called epigrams come fifteen **Sonnets**, eleven of which are easily recognisable amongst the **Visions of Bellay**, published along with the Visions of Petrarch. There is indeed as little difference between the two sets of poems as is compatible with the fact that the old series is written in blank verse, the latter in rhyme. The sonnets which appear for the first time in the **Visions** are those describing the Wolf, the River, the Vessel, the City. There are four pieces of the older series which are not reproduced in the later. It would seem probable that they too may have been written by Spenser in the days of his youth, though at a later period of his life he cancelled and superseded them. They are therefore reprinted in this volume. (See pp. 699-701.)

Vander Noodt, it must be said, makes no mention of Spenser in his volume. It would seem that he did not know English, and that he wrote his **Declaration**--a sort of commentary in prose on the **Visions**--in French. At least we are told that this **Declaration** is translated out of French into English by Theodore Roest. All that is stated of the origin of his **Visions** is: 'The learned poete M. Francisce Petrarche, gentleman of Florence, did invent and write in Tuscan the six firste . . . . which because they serve wel to our purpose, I have out of the Brabants speache turned them into the English tongue;' and 'The other ten visions next ensuing ar described of one Ioachim du Bellay, gentleman of France, the whiche also, because they serve to our purpose I have translated them out of Dutch into English.' The fact of the *Visions* being subsequently ascribed to Spenser would not by itself carry much weight. But, as Prof. Craik pertinently asks, 'if this English version was not the work of Spenser, where did Ponsonby [the printer who issued that subsequent publication which has been mentioned] procure the corrections which are not mere typographical errata, and the additions and other variations{3} that are found in his edition?'

In a work called *Tragical Tales*, published in 1587, there is a letter in verse, dated 1569, addressed to 'Spencer' by George Turberville, then resident in Russia as secretary to the English ambassador, Sir Thomas Randolph. Anthony {a\} Wood says this Spencer was the poet; but it can scarcely have been so. 'Turberville himself,' remarks Prof. Craik, 'is supposed to have been at this time in his twenty-ninth or thirtieth year, which is not the age at which men choose boys of sixteen for their friends. Besides, the verses seem to imply a friendship of some standing, and also in the person addressed the habits and social position of manhood. . . . It has not been commonly noticed that this epistle from Russia is not Turberville's only poetical address to his friend Spencer. Among his "Epitaphs and Sonnets" are two other pieces of verse addressed to the same person.'

To the year 1569 belongs that mention referred to above of payment made one 'Edmund Spenser' for bearing letters from France. As has been already remarked, it is scarcely probable that this can have been the poet, then a youth of some seventeen years on the verge of his undergraduateship.

The one certain event of Spenser's life in the year 1569 is that he was then entered as a sizar at

Pembroke Hall, Cambridge. He 'proceeded B.A.' in 1573,
and 'commenced M.A.' in 1576. There is some reason for
believing that his college life was troubled in much
the same way as was that of Milton some sixty years
later--that there prevailed some misunderstanding
between him and the scholastic authorities. He
mentions his university with respect in the Faerie
Queene, in book iv. canto xi. where, setting forth
what various rivers gathered happily together to
celebrate the marriage of the Thames and the Medway, he
tells how

> ... the plenteous Ouse came far from land
> By many a city and by many a towne,
> And many rivers taking under hand
> Into his waters, as he passeth downe,
> The Cle, the Were, the Grant, the Sture, the Rowne.
> Thence doth by Huntingdon and Cambridge flit,
> My mother Cambridge, whom as with a Crowne
> He doth adorne, and is adorn'd of it
>   With many a gentle Muse, and many a learned wit.

But he makes no mention of his college. The notorious
Gabriel Harvey, an intimate friend of Spenser, who was
elected a Fellow of Pembroke Hall the year after the
future poet was admitted as a sizar, in a letter
written in 1580, asks: 'And wil you needes have my
testimoniall of youre old Controllers new behaviour?'
and then proceeds to heap abusive words on some person
not mentioned by name but evidently only too well known
to both the sender and the receiver of the epistle.
Having compiled a list of scurrilities worthy of
Falstaff, and attacked another matter which was an

abomination to him, Harvey vents his wrath in sundry
Latin charges, one of which runs: 'C{ae}tera fer{e\}, ut
olim: Bellum inter capita et membra continuatum.'
'Other matters are much as they were: war kept up
between the heads [the dons] and the members [the
men].' Spenser was not elected to a fellowship; he
quitted his college, with all its miserable bickerings,
after he had taken his master's degree. There can be
little doubt, however, that he was most diligent and
earnest student during his residence at Cambridge;
during that period, for example, he must have gained
that knowledge of Plato's works which so distinctly
marks his poems, and found in that immortal writer a
spirit most truly congenial. But it is conceivable
that he pursued his studies after his own manner, and
probably enough excited by his independence the strong
disapprobation of the master and tutor of the college
of his day.

Among his contemporaries in his own college were
Lancelot Andrews, afterwards Master, and eventually
Bishop of Winchester, the famous preacher; Gabriel
Harvey, mentioned above, with whom he formed a fast
friendship, and Edward Kirke, the 'E.K.' who, as will
be seen, introduced to the world Spenser's first work
of any pretence. Amongst his contemporaries in the
university were Preston, author of ***Cambyses***, and
Still, author of ***Gammer Gurtons Needle***, with each of
whom he was acquainted. The friend who would seem to
have exercised the most influence over him was Gabriel
Harvey; but this influence, at least in literary
matters, was by no means for the best. Harvey was some
three or four years the senior, and of some academic
distinction. Probably he may be taken as something

more than a fair specimen of the average scholarship and culture given by the universities at that time. He was an extreme classicist; all his admiration was for classical models and works that savoured of them; he it was who headed the attempt made in England to force upon a modern language the metrical system of the Greeks and Latins. What baneful influence he exercised over Spenser in this last respect will be shown presently. Kirke was Spenser's other close friend; he was one year junior academically to the poet. He too, as we shall see, was a profound admirer of Harvey.

After leaving the university in 1576, Spenser, then, about twenty-four years of age, returned to his own people in the North. This fact is learnt from his friend 'E.K.'s' glosses to certain lines in the sixth book of the **Shepheardes Calendar**. E.K. speaks 'of the North countrye where he dwelt,' and 'of his removing out of the North parts and coming into the South.' As E.K. writes in the spring of 1579, and as his writing is evidently some little time subsequent to the migration he speaks of, it may be believed that Spenser quitted his Northern home in 1577, and, as we shall see, there is other evidence for this supposition. About a year then was passed in the North after he left the University.

These years were not spent idly. The poetical fruits of them shall be mentioned presently. What made it otherwise a memorable year to the poet was his falling deeply in love with some fair Northern neighbour. Who she was is not known. He who adored her names her Rosalind, 'a feigned name,' notes E.K., 'which being well ordered will bewray the very name of hys love and mistresse, whom by that name he

coloureth.' Many solutions of this anagram have been
essayed, mostly on the supposition that the lady lived
in Kent; but Professor Craik is certainly right in
insisting that she was of the North. Dr. Grosart and
Mr. Fleay, both authorities of importance, agree in
discovering the name Rose Dinle or Dinley; but of a
person so Christian-named no record has yet been found,
though the surname Dyneley or Dinley occurs in the
Whalley registers and elsewhere. In the Eclogue of the
Shepheardes Calendar, to which this note is appended,
Colin Clout--so the poet designates himself--complains
to Hobbinol--that is, Harvey -of the ill success of his
passion. Harvey, we may suppose, is paying him a visit
in the North; or perhaps the pastoral is merely a
versifying of what passed between them in letters.
However this may be, Colin is bewailing his hapless
fate. His friend, in reply, advises him to

Forsake the soyle that so doth thee bewitch, &c.

Surely E.K.'s gloss is scarcely necessary to tell us
what these words mean. 'Come down,' they say, 'from
your bleak North country hills where she dwells who
binds you with her spell, and be at peace far away from
her in the genial South land.' In another Eclogue
(April) the subduing beauty is described as 'the
Widdowes daughter of the Glen,' surely a Northern
address. On these words the well-informed E.K.
remarks: 'He calleth Rosalind the Widowes daughter of
the glenne, that is, of a country hamlet or borough,
which I thinke is rather sayde to coloure and concele
the person, than simply spoken. For it is well known,
even in spighte of Colin and Hobbinol, that she is a

gentlewoman of no meane house, nor endowed with anye vulgare and common gifts, both of nature and manners: but suche indeede, as neede neither Colin be ashamed to have her made known by his verses, nor Hobbinol be greved that so she should be commended to immortalitie for her rare and singular virtues.' Whoever this charming lady was, and whatever glen she made bright with her presence, it appears that she did not reciprocate the devoted affection of the studious young Cambridge graduate who, with probably no apparent occupation, was loitering for a while in her vicinity. It was some other--he is called Menalacas in one of his rival's pastorals--who found favour in her eyes. The poet could only wail and beat his breast. Eclogues I. and VI. are all sighs and tears. Perhaps in the course of time a copy of the **Faerie Queene** might reach the region where Menalcas and Rosalind were growing old together; and she, with a certain ruth perhaps mixed with her anger, might recognise in Mirabella an image of her fair young disdainful self{4}. The poet's attachment was no transient flame that flashed and was gone. When at the instance of his friend he travelled southward away from the scene of his discomfiture, he went weeping and inconsolable. In the Fourth Eclogue Hobbinol is discovered by Thenot deeply mourning, and, asked the reason, replies that his grief is because

. . . the ladde whome long I loved so deare
Nowe loves a lasse that all his love doth scorne;
  He plongd in payne, his tressed locks dooth teare.

Shepheards delights he dooth them all forsweare;
  Hys pleasant pipe, whych made us meriment,

He wylfully hath broke, and doth forbeare
   His wonted songs, wherein he all outwent.

·   ·   ·   ·   ·

Colin thou kenst, the Southerne shepheardes boye;
   Him Love hath wounded with a deadly darte. &c.

The memory of Rosalind, in spite of her unkindness,
seems to have been fondly cherished by the poet, and
yielded to no rival vision--though there may have been
fleeting fits of passion--till some fourteen years
after he and she had parted--till the year 1592, when,
as we shall see, Spenser, then living in the south of
Ireland, met that Elizabeth who is mentioned in the
sonnet quoted above, and who some year and a half after
that meeting became his wife. On the strength of an
entry found in the register of St. Clement Danes Church
in the Strand--'26 Aug. [1587] Florenc Spenser, the
daughter of Edmond'--it has been conjectured that the
poet was married before 1587. This conjecture seems
entirely unacceptable. There is nothing to justify the
theory that the Edmund Spenser of the register was the
poet. It is simply incredible that Spenser, one who,
as has been said, poured out all his soul in his poems,
should have wooed and won some fair lady to his wife,
without ever a poetical allusion to his courtship and
his triumph. It is not at all likely, as far as one
can judge from their titles, that any one of his lost
works was devoted to the celebration of any such
successful passion. Lastly, besides this important
negative evidence, there is distinct positive testimony
that long after 1587 the image of Rosalind had not been

displaced in his fancy by any other loveliness. In
Colin Clouts Come Home Again, written, as will be
seen, in 1591, though not published until 1595, after
the poet has 'full deeply divined of love and beauty,'
one Melissa in admiration avers that all true lovers
are greatly bound to him--most especially women. The
faithful Hobbinol says that women have but ill requited
their poet:--

   'He is repayd with scorne and foule despite,
   That yrkes each gentle heart which it doth heare.'
   'Indeed,' says Lucid, 'I have often heard
   Faire Rosalind of divers fowly blamed
   For being to that swaine too cruell hard.

Lucid however would defend her on the ground that love
may not be compelled:--

   'Beware therefore, ye groomes, I read betimes
   How rashly blame of Rosalind ye raise.'

This caution Colin eagerly and ardently reinforces, and
with additions. His heart was still all tender towards
her, and he would not have one harsh word thrown at
her:--

   Ah! Shepheards, then said Colin, ye ne weet
   How great a guilt upon your heads ye draw
   To make so bold a doome, with words unmeet,
   Of thing celestiall which ye never saw.
   For she is not like as the other crew
   Of shepheards daughters which emongst you bee,
   But of divine regard and heavenly hew,

Excelling all that ever ye did see;
Not then to her that scorned thing so base,
But to myselfe the blame that lookt so hie,
So hie her thoughts as she herselfe have place
And loath each lowly thing with lofty eie;
Yet so much grace let her vouchsafe to grant
To simple swaine, sith her I may not love,
Yet that I may her honour paravant
And praise her worth, though far my wit above.
Such grace shall be some guerdon for the griefe
And long affliction which I have endured;
Such grace sometimes shall give me some reliefc
And ease of paine which cannot be recured.
And ye my fellow shepheards, which do see
And heare the languors of my too long dying,
Unto the world for ever witnesse bee
That hers I die, nought to the world denying
This simple trophe of her great conquest.

This residence of Spenser in the North, which
corresponds with that period of Milton's life spent at
his father's house at Horton in Buckinghamshire, ended,
as there has been occasion to state, in the year 1577.
What was the precise cause of Spenser's coming South,
is not known for certain. 'E.K.' says in one of his
glosses, already quoted in part, that the poet 'for
speciall occasion of private affayres (as I have bene
partly of himselfe informed) and for his more
preferment, removing out of the North parts, came into
the South, as Hobbinoll indeede advised him privately.'
It is clear from his being admitted at his college as a
sizar, that his private means were not good. Perhaps
during his residence in the North he may have been

dependent on the bounty of his friends. It was then in
the hope of some advancement of his fortunes that,
bearing with him no doubt in manuscript certain results
of all his life's previous labour, he turned away from
his cold love and her glen, and all her country, and
set his face Town-ward.

It is said that his friend Harvey introduced him
to that famous accomplished gentleman--that mirror of
true knighthood--Sir Philip Sidney, and it would seem
that Penshurst became for some time his home. There
has already been quoted a line describing Spenser as
'the southern shepheardes boye.' This southern
shepherd is probably Sidney. Sidney, it would seem,
introduced him to his father and to his uncle, the Earl
of Leicester. If we are to take Iren{ae}us' words
literally--and there seems no reason why we should
not--Spenser was for a time at least in Ireland, when
Sidney's father was Lord Deputy. Iren{ae}us, in A View
of the Present State of Ireland, certainly represents
Spenser himself; and he speaks of what he *said* at the
execution of a notable traitor at Limerick, called
Murrogh O'Brien; see p. 636 of this volume. However,
he was certainly back in England and in London in 1579,
residing at the Earl of Leicester's house in the
Strand, where Essex Street now stands. He dates one of
his letters to Harvey, 'Leycester House, this 5
October, 1579.' Perhaps at this time he commenced, or
renewed, or continued his acquaintance with his
distinguished relatives at Althorpe. During the time
he spent now at Penshurst and in London, he mixed
probably with the most brilliant intellectual society
of his time. Sidney was himself endowed with no mean
genius. He, Lord Leicester, Lord Strange, and others,

with whom Spenser was certainly, or in all probability, acquainted, were all eminent patrons and protectors of genius.

This passage of Spenser's life is of high interest, because in the course of it that splendid era of our literature commonly called the Elizabethan Period may be said to have begun. Spenser is the foremost chronologically of those great spirits who towards the close of the sixteenth century lifted up their immortal voices, and spoke words to be heard for all time. In the course of this present passage of his life, he published his first important work--a work which secured him at once the hearty recognition of his contemporaries as a true poet risen up amongst them. This work was the **Shepheardes Calendar**, to which so many references have already been made.

It consists of twelve eclogues, one for each month of the year. Of these, three (i., vi., and xii.), as we have seen, treat specially of his own disappointment in love. Three (ii., viii., and x.) are of a more general character, having old age, a poetry combat, 'the perfect pattern of a poet' for their subjects. One other (iii.) deals with love-matters. One (iv.) celebrates the Queen, three (v., vii, and ix.) discuss 'Protestant and Catholic,' Anglican and Puritan questions. One (xi.) is an elegy upon 'the death of some maiden of great blood, whom he calleth Dido.' These poems were ushered into the world by Spenser's college friend Edward Kirke, for such no doubt is the true interpretation of the initials E.K. This gentleman performed his duty in a somewhat copious manner. He addressed 'to the most excellent and learned both orator and poet Mayster Gabriell Harvey' a letter warmly commending 'the new poet' to his patronage, and defending the antique verbiage of the eclogues; he prefixed to the whole work a general argument, a particular one to each part; he appended to every poem a 'glosse' explaining words and allusions. The work is dedicated to Sir Philip Sidney. It was published in the winter of 1579-80.

More than once in the course of it, Spenser refers to Tityrus as his great master. The twelfth eclogue opens thus:

The gentle shepheard sat beside a springe
  All in the shadow of a bushye brere,
That Colin height, which well could pype and singe,
  For hee of Tityrus his songs did lere.

Tityrus, on E.K.'s authority, was Chaucer. It is evident from the language--both the words and verbal forms--used in this poem that Spenser had zealously studied Chaucer, whose greatest work had appeared just about two centuries before Spenser's first important publication. The work, however, in which he imitates Chaucer's manner is not the *Shepheardes Calendar*, but his *Prosopopoia or Mother Hubberds Tale*, which he says, writing in a later year, he had 'long sithens composed in the raw conceipt of my youth.' The form and manner of the *Shepheardes Calendar* reflected not Chaucer's influence upon the writer, but the influence of a vast event which had changed the face of literature since the out-coming of the Canterbury Tales--of the revival of learning. That event had put fresh models before men, had greatly modified old literary forms, had originated new. The classical influence impressed upon Europe was by no means an unmixed good; in some respects it retarded the natural development of the modern mind by overpowering it with its prestige and stupefying it with a sense of inferiority; while it raised the ideal of perfection, it tended to give rise to mere imitations and affectations. Amongst these new forms was the Pastoral. When Virgil, Theocritus, 'Daphnis and Chloe,' and other writers and works of the ancient pastoral literature once more gained the ascendancy, then a modern pastoral poetry began to be. This poetry flourished greatly in Italy in the sixteenth century. It had been cultivated by Sannazaro, Guarini, Tasso. Arcadia had been adopted by the poets for their country. In England numerous *Eclogues* made their appearance. Amongst the earliest and the best of these were Spenser's. It would perhaps be unjust to treat this modern pastoral literature as altogether an affectation. However unreal, the pastoral world had its charms--a pleasant feeling imparted of emancipation, a deep quietude, a sweet tranquillity. If vulgar men discovered their new worlds, and trafficked and bustled there, why should not the poet discover his Arcadia, and repose at his ease in it, secure from the noises of feet coming and going over the roads of the earth?

   That fine melodiousness, which is one of Spenser's signal characteristics, may be perceived in his *Eclogues*, as also a native gracefulness of style, which is another distinguishing mark of him. Perceivable, too, are his great, perilous fluency of language and his immense fecundity of mind. The work at once secured him a front place in the poetical ranks of the day. Sidney mentions it in his Apologie for Poetrie;{5} Abraham Fraunce draws illustrations from it in his *Lawyers Logicke*, which appeared in 1588; Meres praises it; 'Maister Edmund Spenser,' says Drayton, 'has done enough for the immortality, had he only given us his *Shepheardes Calendar*, a masterpiece, if any.' It is easy to discern in *Lycidas* signs of Milton's study of it.

During Spenser's sojourn in the society of the Sidneys and the Dudleys, letters passed between him and Harvey, some of which are extant. From these, and from the editorial notes of Kirke, we hear of other works written by Spenser, ready to be given to the light. The works thus heard of are *Dreames*, *Legends*, *Court of Cupide*, *The English Poet*, The Dying Pelican, Stemmata Dudleiana, Slomber, Nine English Comedies, The Epithalamion Thamesis, and also *The Faerie Queene* commenced. Of these works perhaps the *Legends*, *Court of Cupide*, and *Epithalamion Thamesis* were subsequently with modifications incorporated in the *Faerie Queene*; the *Stemmata Dudleiana*, *Nine English Comedies*, Dying Pelican, *are altogether lost. The* Faerie Queene had been begun. So far as written, it had been submitted to the criticism of Harvey. On April 10, 1580, Spenser writes to Harvey, wishing him to return it with his 'long expected judgment' upon it. Harvey had already pronounced sentence in a letter dated April 7, and this is the sentence: 'In good faith I had once again nigh forgotten your *Faerie Queene*; howbeit, by good chaunce I have nowe sent hir home at the laste, neither in a better nor worse case than I founde hir. And must

you of necessitie have my judgement of hir indeede? To
be plaine, I am voyde of al judgement, if your nine
Com{oe}dies, whereunto, in imitation of Herodotus, you
give the names of the Nine Muses, and (in one man's
fansie not unworthily), come not neerer Ariostoes
Com{oe}dies, eyther for the finenesse of plausible
elocution, or the rareness of poetical invention, than
that Elvish queene doth to his Orlando Furioso, which
notwithstanding, you will needes seem to emulate, and
hope to overgo, as you flatly professed yourself in one
of your last letters. Besides that, you know it hath
bene the usual practise of the most exquisite and odde
wittes in all nations, and especially in Italie, rather
to shewe and advaunce themselves that way than any
other; as namely, those three notorious dyscoursing
heads Bibiena, Machiavel, and Aretine did (to let Bembo
and Ariosto passe), with the great admiration and
wonderment of the whole countrey; being indeede reputed
matchable in all points, both for conceyt of witte, and
eloquent decyphering of matters, either with
Aristophanes and Menander in Greek, or with Plautus and
Terence in Latin, or with any other in any other tong.
But I will not stand greatly with you in your owne
matters. If so be the Faery Queen be fairer in your
eie than the Nine Muses, and Hobgoblin runne away with
the garland from Apollo; marke what I saye, and yet I
will not say that I thought; but there is an end for
this once, and fare you well, till God or some good
Aungell putte you in a better minde.'

Clearly the *Faerie Queene* was but little to
Harvey's taste. It was too alien from the cherished
exemplars of his heart. Happily Spenser was true to
himself, and went on with his darling work in spite of

the strictures of pedantry. This is not the only
instance in which the dubious character of Harvey's
influence is noticeable. The letters, from one of
which the above doom is quoted, enlighten us also as to
a grand scheme entertained at this time for forcing the
English tongue to conform to the metrical rules of the
classical languages. Already in a certain circle rime
was discredited as being, to use Milton's words nearly
a century afterwards, 'no necessary adjunct or true
ornament of poem or good verse, in longer works
especially, but the invention of a barbarous age to set
off wretched matter and lame metre.' A similar attempt
was made in the course of the sixteenth century in
other parts of Europe, and with the same final issue.
Gabriel Harvey was an active leader in this deluded
movement. When Sidney too, and Dyer, another poet of
the time, proclaimed a 'general surceasing and silence
of bald rhymes, and also of the very best too, instead
whereof they have by authority of their whole senate,
prescribed certain laws and rules of quantity of
English syllables for English verse, having had already
thereof great practice,' Spenser was drawn 'to their
faction.'

'I am of late,' he writes to Harvey, 'more in love
wyth my Englishe versifying than with ryming; whyche I
should have done long since if I would then have
followed your councell.' In allying himself with these
Latin prosody bigots Spenser sinned grievously against
his better taste. 'I like your late Englishe
hexameters so exceedingly well,' he writes to Harvey,
'that I also enure my pen sometime in that kinde,
whyche I find in deed, as I have heard you often
defende in word, neither so harde nor so harsh [but]

that it will easily and fairly yield itself to our
mother tongue. For the onely or chiefest hardnesse
whyche seemeth is in the accente; whyche sometimes
gapeth and as it were yawneth il-favouredly, comming
shorte of that it should, and sometimes exceeding the
measure of the number; as in carpenter the middle
sillable being used short in speache, when it shall be
read long in verse, seemeth like a lame gosling that
draweth one legge after hir. And heaven being used
shorte as one syllable, when it is in verse stretched
with a Diastole is like a lame dogge, that holdes up
one legge.'{6} His ear was far too fine and sensitive
to endure the fearful sounds uttered by the poets of
this Procrust{ae}an creed. The language seemed to groan
and shriek at the agonies and contortions to which it
was subjected; and Spenser could not but hear its
outcries. But he made himself as deaf as might be.
'It is to be wonne with custom,' he proceeds, in the
letter just quoted from, 'and rough words must be
studied with use. For why, a God's name, may not we,
as the Greekes, have the kingdom of oure owne language,
and measure our accentes by the sounde, reserving the
quantitie to the verse? . . . I would hartily wish you
would either send me the rules or precepts of arte
which you observe in quantities; or else follow mine
that Mr. Philip Sidney gave me, being the very same
which Mr. Drant devised, but enlarged with Mr. Sidney's
own judgement, and augmented with my observations, that
we might both accorde and agree in one, leaste we
overthrowe one another and be overthrown of the rest.'
He himself produced the following lines in accordance,
as he fondly hoped, with the instructions of the new
school:--

IAMBICUM TRIMETRUM.

Unhappie verse! the witnesse of my unhappie state,
[as indeed it was in a sense not meant]
Make thy selfe fluttring winge of thy fast flying
thought,
And fly forth unto my love whersoever she be.

Whether lying reastlesse in heavy bedde, or else
Sitting so cheerelesse at the cheerefull boorde, or
else
Playing alone carelesse on hir heavenlie virginals.

If in bed, tell hir that my eyes can take no reste;
If at boorde, tell hir that my mouth can eat no
meete;
If at hir virginals, tell her I can beare no mirth.

Asked why? Waking love suffereth no sleepe;
Say that raging love doth appall the weake stomacke,
Say that lamenting love marreth the musicall.

Tell hir that hir pleasures were wonte to lull me
asleepe,
Tell her that hir beauty was wonte to fecde mine
eyes,
Tell hir that hir sweete tongue was wonte to make me
mirth.

Now doe I nightly waste, wanting my kindlie rest,
Now doe I dayly starve, wanting my daily food,
Now doe I always dye wanting my timely mirth.

And if I waste who will bewaile my heavy chance?
And if I starve, who will record my cursed end?
And if I dye, who will saye, This was Immerito?

Spenser of the sensitive ear wrote these lines. When
the pedantic phantasy which had for a while seduced and
corrupted him had gone from him, with what remorse he
must have remembered these strange monsters of his
creation! Let us conclude our glance at this sad fall
from harmony by quoting the excellent words of one who
was a bitter opponent of Harvey in this as in other
matters. 'The hexameter verse,' says Nash in his
Fowre Letters Confuted, 1592, 'I graunt to be a
gentleman of an auncient house (so is many an English
beggar), yet this clyme of ours hee cannot thrive in;
our speech is too craggy for him to set his plough in;
hee goes twitching and hopping in our language like a
man running upon quagmiers up the hill in one syllable
and down the dale in another; retaining no part of that
stately smooth gate, which he vaunts himselfe with
amongst the Greeks and Latins.'

Some three years were spent by Spenser in the
enjoyment of Sidney's friendship and the patronage of
Sidney's father and uncle. During this time he would
seem to have been constantly hoping for some
preferment. According to a tradition, first recorded
by Fuller, the obstructor of the success of his suit
was the Treasurer, Lord Burghley. It is clear that he
had enemies at Court--at least at a later time. In
1591, in his dedication of Colin Clouts Come Home
Again, he entreats Raleigh, to 'with your good
countenance protest against the malice of evil mouthes,

which are always wide open to carpe at and misconstrue
my simple meaning.' A passage in the **Ruines of Time**
(see the lines beginning 'O grief of griefs! O full of
all good hearts!') points to the same conclusion; and
so the concluding lines of the Sixth Book of the
Faerie Queene, when, having told how the Blatant
Beast (not killed as Lord Macaulay says in his essay on
Bunyan, but 'supprest and tamed' for a while by Sir
Calidore) at last broke his iron chain and ranged again
through the world, and raged sore in each degree and
state, he adds:--

> Ne may this homely verse, of many meanest,
>   Hope to escape his venemous despite,
> More then my former writs, all were they clearest
>   From blamefull blot, and from all that wite,
> With which some wicked tongues did it backebite,
> And bring into a mighty Peres displeasure,
> That never so deserved to endite.
> Therfore do you my rimes keep better measure,
>   And seek to please, that now is counted wisemens
> threasure.

In the **Tears of the Muses** Calliope says of certain
persons of eminent rank:--

> Their great revenues all in sumptuous pride
> They spend that nought to learning they may spare;
> And the rich fee which Poets wont divide
> Now Parasites and Sycophants do share.

Several causes have been suggested to account for this
disfavour. The popular tradition was pleased to

explain it by making Burghley the ideal dullard who has
no soul for poetry--to whom one copy of verses is very
much as good as another, and no copy good for anything.
It delighted to bring this commonplace gross-minded
person into opposition with one of the most spiritual
of geniuses. In this myth Spenser represents mind,
Burghley matter. But there is no justification in
facts for this tradition. It may be that the Lord
Treasurer was not endowed with a high intellectual
nature; but he was far too wise in his generation not
to pretend a virtue if he had it not, when
circumstances called for anything of the sort. When
the Queen patronized literature, we may be sure Lord
Burghley was too discreet to disparage and oppress it.
Another solution refers to Burghley's Puritanism as the
cause of the misunderstanding; but, as Spenser too
inclined that way, this is inadequate. Probably, as
Todd and others have thought, what alienated his
Lordship at first was Spenser's connection with
Leicester; what subsequently aggravated the
estrangement was his friendship with Essex.

Notes

{1} See Peter Cunningham's Introduction to Extracts
    from Accounts of the Revels at Court. (Shakspeare
    Society.)
{2} It may be suggested that what are called the
    archaisms of Spenser's style may be ***in part*** due
    to the author's long residence in the country with

one of the older forms of the language spoken all round him and spoken by him, in fact his vernacular. I say *in part*, because of course his much study of Chaucer must be taken into account. But, as Mr. Richard Morris has remarked to me, he could not have drawn from Chaucer those forms and words of a *northern* dialect which appear in the *Calendar*.

{3} These are given in the Appendix to the present work.

{4} This supposed description of his first love was written probably during the courtship, which ended, as we shall see, in his marriage. The First Love is said to be portrayed in cant. vii., the Last in cant. x. of book vi. of the *Faerie Queene*. But this identification of Rosalind and Mirabilla is, after all, but a conjecture, and is not be accepted as gospel.

{5} See this work amongst Mr. Arber's excellent *English Reprints*.

{6} *Ancient Critical Essays*, ed. Hazlewood, 1815, pp. 259, 260.

CHAPTER II.

1580-1589.

In the year 1580 Spenser was removed from the society
and circumstances in which, except for his probable
visit to Ireland, he had lived and moved as we have
seen, for some three years. From that year to near the
close of his life his home was to be in Ireland. He
paid at least two visits to London and its environs in
the course of these eighteen years; but it seems clear
that his home was in Ireland. Perhaps his biographers
have hitherto not truly appreciated this residence in
Ireland. We shall see that a liberal grant of land was
presently bestowed upon him in the county of Cork; and
they have reckoned him a successful man, and wondered
at the querulousness that occasionally makes itself
heard in his works. Towards the very end of this life,
Spenser speaks of himself as one

> Whom sullein care
> Through discontent of my long fruitlesse stay
> In princes court and expectation vayne
> Of idle hopes, which still doe fly away
> Like empty shaddowes, did afflict my brayne.

Those who marvel at such language perhaps forget what a
dreary exile the poet's life in Ireland must in fact
have been. It is true that it was relieved by several
journeys to England, by his receiving at least one

visit from an English friend, by his finding, during at
any rate the earlier part of his absence, some
congenial English friends residing in the country, by
his meeting at length with that Elizabeth whose
excelling beauty he has sung so sweetly, and whom he
married; it is also true that there was in him--as in
Milton and in Wordsworth--a certain great self-
containedness,{1} that he carried his world with him
wherever he went, that he had great allies and high
company in the very air that flowed around him,
whatever land he inhabited; all this is true, but yet
to be cut off from the fellowship which, however self-
sufficing, he so dearly loved--to look no longer on the
face of Sidney his hero, his ideal embodied, his living
Arthur, to hear but as it were an echo of the splendid
triumphs won by his and our England in those glorious
days, to know of his own high fame but by report, to be
parted from the friendship of Shakspere--surely this
was exile. To live in the Elizabethan age, and to be
severed from those brilliant spirits to which the fame
of that age is due! Further, the grievously unsettled,
insurgent state of Ireland at this time--as at many a
time before and since--must be borne in mind. Living
there was living on the side of a volcanic mountain.
That the perils of so living were not merely imaginary,
we shall presently see. He did not shed tears and
strike his bosom, like the miserable Ovid at Tomi; he
'wore rather in his bonds a cheerful brow, lived, and
took comfort,' finding his pleasure in that high
spiritual communion we have spoken of, playing
pleasantly, like some happy father, with the children
of his brain, joying in their caprices, their
noblenesses, their sweet adolescence; but still it was

exile, and this fact may explain that tone of discontent which here and there is perceptible in his writings.{2}

When in 1580 Arthur, Lord Grey of Wilton, was appointed Lord Deputy of Ireland, he--perhaps through Lord Leicester's influence, perhaps on account of Spenser's already knowing something of the country--made Spenser his Private Secretary. There can be no doubt that Spenser proceeded with him to Dublin. It was in Ireland, probably about this time, that he made or renewed his acquaintance with Sir Walter Raleigh. In 1581 he was appointed Clerk of Degrees and Recognizances in the Irish Court of Chancery, a post which he held for seven years, at the end of which time he received the appointment of Clerk to the Council of Munster. In the same year in which he was assigned the former clerkship, he received also a lease of the lands and Abbey of Enniscorthy in Wexford county. It is to be hoped that his Chancery Court duties permitted him to reside for a while on that estate. 'Enniscorthy,' says the *Guide to Ireland* published by Mr. Murray, 'is one of the prettiest little towns in the Kingdom, the largest portion of it being on a steep hill on the right bank of the Slaney, which here becomes a deep and navigable stream, and is crossed by a bridge of six arches.' There still stands there 'a single tower of the old Franciscan monastery.' But Spenser soon parted with this charming spot, perhaps because of its inconvenient distance from the scene of his official work. In December of the year in which the lease was given, he transferred it to one Richard Synot. In the following year Lord Grey was recalled. 'The Lord Deputy,' says Holinshed, 'after long suit for his

revocation, received Her Majesty's letters for the
same.' His rule had been marked by some extreme,
perhaps necessary, severities, and was probably
somewhat curtly concluded on account of loud complaints
made against him on this score. Spenser would seem to
have admired and applauded him, both as a ruler and as
a patron and friend. He mentions him with much respect
in his *View of the Present State of Ireland*. One of
the sonnets prefixed to the *Faerie Queene* is
addressed 'to the most renowmed and valiant lord the
lord Grey of Wilton,' and speaks of him with profound
gratitude:--

Most noble lord the pillor of my life,
And patrone of my Muses pupillage,
Through whose large bountie poured on me rife,
In the first season of my feeble age,
I now doe live, bound yours by vassalage:
Sith nothing ever may redeeme, nor reave
Out of your endlesse debt so sure a gage,
Vouchsafe in worth this small guift to receave,
Which in your noble hands for pledge I leave,
Of all the rest, that I am tyde t' account.

Lord Grey died in 1593. Spenser may have renewed his
friendship with him in 1589, when, as we shall see, he
visited England. For the present their connection was
broken. It may be considered as fairly certain that
when his lordship returned to England in 1582, Spenser
did not return with him, but abode still in Ireland.

There is, indeed, a 'Maister Spenser' mentioned in
a letter written by James VI. of Scotland from St.
Andrews in 1583 to Queen Elizabeth: 'I have staied

Maister Spenser upon the letter quhilk is written with
my auin hand quhilk sall be readie within tua daies.'
It may be presumed that this gentleman is the same with
him of whose postal services mention is found, as we
have seen, in 1569. At any rate there is nothing
whatever to justify his identification with the poet.
On the other hand, there are several circumstances
which seem to indicate that Spenser was in Ireland
continuously from the year of his going there with Lord
Grey to the year of his visiting England with Raleigh
in 1589, when he presented to her Majesty and published
the first three books of the *Faerie Queene*. Whatever
certain glimpses we can catch of Spenser during these
ten years, he is in Ireland.

We have seen that he was holding one clerkship or
another in Ireland during all this time. In the next
place, we find him mentioned as forming one of a
company described as gathered together at a cottage
near Dublin in a work by his friend Lodovick{3}
Bryskett, written, as may be inferred with considerable
certainty, some time in or about the year 1582, though
not published till 1606. This work, entitled A
Discourse of Civill Life; containing the Ethike part of
Morall Philosophie, 'written to the right honorable
Arthur, late Lord Grey of Wilton'--written before his
recall in 1582--describes in the introduction a party
met together at the author's cottage near Dublin,
consisting of 'Dr. Long, Primate of Ardmagh; Sir Robert
Dillon, knight; M. Dormer, the Queene's sollicitor;
Capt. Christopher Carleil; Capt. Thomas Norreis; Capt.
Warham St. Leger; Capt. Nicholas Dawtrey; and M. Edmond
Spenser, late your lordship's secretary; and Th. Smith,
apothecary.' In the course of conversation Bryskett

envies 'the happinesse of the Italians who have in
their mother-tongue late writers that have with a
singular easie method taught all that which Plato or
Aristotle have confusedly or obscurely left written.'
The 'late writers' who have performed this highly
remarkable service of clarifying and making
intelligible Plato and Aristotle--perhaps the
'confusion' and 'obscurity' Bryskett speaks of mean
merely the difficulties of a foreign language for one
imperfectly acquainted with it--are Alexander
Piccolomini, Gio. Baptista Giraldi, and Guazzo, 'all
three having written upon the Ethick part of Morall
Philosopie [sic] both exactly and perspicuously.'
Bryskett then earnestly wishes--and here perhaps, in
spite of those queer words about Plato and Aristotle,
we may sympathise with him--that some of our countrymen
would promote by English treatises the study of Moral
Philosophy in English.

'In the meane while I must struggle with those
bookes which I vnderstand and content myselfe to
plod upon them, in hope that God (who knoweth the
sincerenesse of my desire) will be pleased to open
my vnderstanding, so as I may reape that profit of
my reading, which I trauell for. Yet is there a
gentleman in this company, whom I have had often a
purpose to intreate, that as his leisure might serue
him, he would vouchsafe to spend some time with me
to instruct me in some hard points which I cannot of
myselfe understand; knowing him to be not onely
perfect in the Greek tongue, but also very well read
in Philosophie, both morall and naturall.
Neuertheless such is my bashfulnes, as I neuer yet

durst open my mouth to disclose this my desire unto
him, though I have not wanted some hartning
thereunto from himselfe. For of loue and kindnes to
me, he encouraged me long sithens to follow the
reading of the Greeke tongue, and offered me his
helpe to make me vnderstand it. But now that so
good an oportunitie is offered vnto me, to satisfie
in some sort my desire; I thinke I should commit a
great fault, not to myselfe alone, but to all this
company, if I should not enter my request thus
farre, as to moue him to spend this time which we
have now destined to familiar discourse and
conuersation, in declaring unto us the great
benefits which men obtaine by knowledge of Morall
Philosophie, and in making us to know what the same
is, what be the parts thereof, whereby vertues are
to be distinguished from vices; and finally that he
will be pleased to run ouer in such order as he
shall thinke good, such and so many principles and
rules thereof, as shall serue not only for my better
instruction, but also for the contentment and
satisfaction of you al. For I nothing doubt, but
that euery one of you will be glad to heare so
profitable a discourse and thinke the time very wel
spent wherin so excellent a knowledge shal be
reuealed unto you, from which euery one may be
assured to gather some fruit as wel as myselfe.
Therefore (said I) turning myselfe to *M. Spenser*,
It is you, sir, to whom it pertaineth to shew
yourselfe courteous now unto us all and to make vs
all beholding unto you for the pleasure and profit
which we shall gather from your speeches, if you
shall vouchsafe to open unto vs the goodly cabinet,

in which this excellent treasure of vertues lieth
locked up from the vulgar sort. And thereof in the
behalfe of all as for myselfe, I do most earnestly
intreate you not to say vs nay. Vnto which wordes
of mine euery man applauding most with like words of
request and the rest with gesture and countenances
expressing as much, *M. Spenser* answered in this
maner: Though it may seeme hard for me, to refuse
the request made by you all, whom euery one alone, I
should for many respects be willing to gratifie; yet
as the case standeth, I doubt not but with the
consent of the most part of you, I shall be excused
at this time of this taske which would be laid vpon
me, for sure I am, that it is not vnknowne unto you,
that I haue already vndertaken a work tending to the
same effect, which is in *heroical verse* under the
title of a *Faerie Queene* to represent all the
moral vertues, assigning to every vertue a Knight to
be the patron and defender of the same, in whose
actions and feates of arms and chiualry the
operations of that vertue, whereof he is the
protector, are to be expressed, and the vices and
unruly appetites that oppose themselves against the
same, to be beaten down and overcome. Which work,
as I haue already well entred into, if God shall
please to spare me life that I may finish it
according to my mind, your wish (*M. Bryskett*) will
be in some sort accomplished, though perhaps not so
effectually as you could desire. And the may very
well serue for my excuse, if at this time I craue to
be forborne in this your request, since any
discourse, that I might make thus on the sudden in
such a subject would be but simple, and little to

your satisfactions. For it would require good
aduisement and premeditation for any man to
vndertake the declaration of these points that you
have proposed, containing in effect the Ethicke part
of Morall Philosophie. Whereof since I haue taken
in hand to discourse at large in my poeme before
spoken, I hope the expectation of that work may
serue to free me at this time from speaking in that
matter, notwithstanding your motion and all your
intreaties. But I will tell you how I thinke by
himselfe he may very well excuse my speech, and yet
satisfie all you in this matter. I haue seene (as
he knoweth) a translation made by himselfe out of
the Italian tongue of a dialogue comprehending all
the Ethick part of Moral Philosophy, written by one
of those three he formerly mentioned, and that is by
Giraldi under the title of a dialogue of ciuil
life. If it please him to bring us forth that
translation to be here read among vs, or otherwise
to deliuer to us, as his memory may serue him, the
contents of the same; he shal (I warrant you)
satisfie you all at the ful, and himselfe wil haue
no cause but to thinke the time well spent in
reuiewing his labors, especially in the company of
so many his friends, who may thereby reape much
profit and the translation happily fare the better
by some mending it may receiue in the perusing, as
all writings else may do by the often examination of
the same. Neither let it trouble him that I so
turne ouer to him againe the taske he wold have put
me to; for it falleth out fit for him to verifie the
principall of all this Apologie, euen now made for
himselfe; because thereby it will appeare that he

hath not withdrawne himselfe from seruice of the
state to live idle or wholly priuate to himselfe,
but hath spent some time in doing that which may
greatly benefit others and hath serued not a little
to the bettering of his owne mind, and increasing of
his knowledge, though he for modesty pretend much
ignorance, and pleade want in wealth, much like some
rich beggars, who either of custom, or for
couetousnes, go to begge of others those things
whereof they haue no want at home. With this answer
of *M. Spensers* it seemed that all the company were
wel satisfied, for after some few speeches whereby
they had shewed an extreme longing after his worke
of the *Faerie Queene*, whereof some parcels had
been by some of them seene, they all began to presse
me to produce my translation mentioned by M.
Spenser that it might be perused among them; or
else that I should (as near as I could) deliuer unto
them the contents of the same, supposing that my
memory would not much faile me in a thing so studied
and advisedly set downe in writing as a translation
must be.'

Bryskett at length assents to Spenser's proposal, and
proceeds to read his translation of Giraldi, which is
in some sort criticised as he reads, Spenser proposing
one or two questions 'arising principally,' as Todd
says, 'from the discussion of the doctrines of Plato
and Aristotle.' This invaluable picture of a scene in
Spenser's Irish life shows manifestly in what high
estimation his learning and genius were already held,
and how, in spite of Harvey's sinister criticisms, he
had resumed his great work. It tells us too that he

found in Ireland a warmly appreciative friend, if
indeed he had not known Bryskett before their going to
Ireland. Bryskett too, perhaps, was acquainted with
Sir Philip Sidney; for two of the elegies written on
that famous knight's death and printed along with
Astrophel in the elegiac collection made by Spenser
were probably of Bryskett's composition, viz., The
Mourning Muse of Thestylis, where 'Liffey's tumbling
stream' is mentioned, and the one entitled A Pastoral
Eclogue, where Lycon offers to 'second' Colin's lament
for Phillisides.

What is said of the *Faerie Queene* in the above
quotation may be illustrated from the sonnet already
quoted from, addressed to Lord Grey--one of the sonnets
that in our modern editions are prefixed to the great
poem. It speaks of the great poem as

> Rude rymes, the which a rustick Muse did weave
> In savadge soyle, far from Parnasso mount.

See also the sonnet addressed to the Right Honourable
the Earl of Ormond and Ossory.

A sonnet addressed to Harvey, is dated 'Dublin
this xviij of July, 1586.' Again, in the course of the
decad now under consideration, Spenser received a grant
of land in Cork--of 3,028 acres, out of the forefeited
estates of the Earl of Desmond.

All these circumstances put together make it
probable, and more than probable, that Spenser remained
in Ireland after Lord Grey's recall. How thorough his
familiarity with the country grew to be, appears from
the work concerning it which he at last produced.

The years 1586-7-8 were eventful both for England

and for Spenser. In the first Sidney expired of wounds
received at Zutphen; in the second, Mary Queen of Scots
was executed; in the third, God blew and scattered the
Armada, and also Leicester died. Spenser weeps over
Sidney--there was never, perhaps, more weeping,
poetical and other, over any death than over that of
Sidney--in his *Astrophel*, the poem above mentioned.
This poem is scarcely worthy of the sad occasion--the
flower of knighthood cut down ere its prime, not yet

>   In flushing
> When blighting was nearest.

Certainly it in no way expresses what Spenser
undoubtedly felt when the woeful news came across the
Channel to him in his Irish home. Probably his grief
was 'too deep for tears.' It was probably one of those
'huge cares' which, in Seneca's phrase, not
'loquuntur,' but 'stupent.' He would fain have been
dumb and opened not his mouth; but the fashion of the
time called upon him to speak. He was expected to
bring his immortelle, so to say, and lay it on his
hero's tomb, though his limbs would scarcely support
him, and his hand, quivering with the agony of his
heart, could with difficulty either weave it or carry
it. All the six years they had been parted, the image
of that chivalrous form had never been forgotten. It
had served for the one model of all that was highest
and noblest in his eyes. It had represented for him
all true knighthood. Nor all the years that he lived
after Sidney's death was it forgotten. It is often
before him, as he writes his later poetry, and is
greeted always with undying love and sorrow. Thus in

the ***Ruines of Time***, he breaks out in a sweet fervour
of unextinguished affection:

> Most gentle spirite breathed from above,
> Out of the bosom of the Makers blis,
> In whom all bountie and all vertuous love
> Appeared in their native propertis
> And did enrich that noble breast of his
> With treasure passing all this worldes worth.
> Worthie of heaven itselfe, which brought it forth.
>
> His blessed spirite, full of power divine
> And influence of all celestiall grace,
> Loathing this sinfull earth and earthlie slime,
> Fled backe too soone unto his native place;
> Too soone for all that did his love embrace,
> Too soone for all this wretched world, whom he
> Robd of all right and true nobilitie.
>
> Yet ere this happie soule to heaven went
> Out of this fleshie gaole, he did devise
> Unto his heavenlie Maker to present
> His bodie as a spotles sacrifise,
> And chose, that guiltie hands of enemies
> Should powre forth th' offring of his guiltles
> blood,
> So life exchanging for his countries good.
>
> O noble spirite, live there ever blessed,
> The world's late wonder, and the heaven's new ioy.
> Live ever there, and leave me here distressed
> With mortall cares and cumbrous worlds anoy;
> But where thou dost that happiness enioy,

Bid me, O bid me quicklie come to thee,
That happie there I maie thee alwaies see.

Yet whilest the Fates affoord me vitell breath,
I will it spend in speaking of thy praise,
And sing to thee untill that timelie death
By Heaven's doome doe ende my earthlie daies:
Thereto doo thou my humble spirite raise,
And into me that sacred breath inspire
Which thou there breathest perfect and entire.

It is not quite certain in what part of Ireland
the poet was living when the news that Sidney was not
reached him. Was he still residing at Dublin, or had
he transferred his home to that southern region which
is so intimately associated with his name? The sonnet
to Harvey mentioned above shows that he was at Dublin
in July of the year of his friend's death. It has been
said already that he did not resign his Chancery
clerkship until 1588. We know that he was settled in
Cork county, at Kilcolman castle, in 1589, because
Raleigh visited him there that year. He may then have
left Dublin in 1588 or 1589. According to Dr. Birch's
Life of Spenser, prefixed to the edition of the Faerie
Queene in 1751,{4} and the **Biographia Britannica**,
the grant of land made him in Cork is dated June 27,
1586. But the grant, which is extant, is dated October
26, 1591. Yet certainly, as Dr. Grosart points out, in
the 'Articles' for the 'Undertakers,' which received
the royal assent on June 27, 1586, Spenser is set down
for 3,028 acres; and that he was at Kilcolman before
1591 seems certain. As he resigned his clerkship in
the Court of Chancery in 1588, and was then appointed,

as we have seen, clerk of the Council of Munster, he
probably went to live somewhere in the province of
Munster that same year. He may have lived at Kilcolman
before it and the surrounding grounds were secured to
him; he may have entered upon possession on the
strength of a promise of them, before the formal grant
was issued. He has mentioned the scenery which
environed his castle twice in his great poem; but it is
worth noticing that both mentions occur, not in the
books published, as we shall now very soon see, in
1590, but in the books published six years afterwards.
In the famous passage already referred to in the
eleventh canto of the fourth book, describing the
nuptials of the Thames and the Medway, he recounts in
stanzas xl.-xliv. the Irish rivers who were present at
that great river-gathering, and amongst them

> Swift Awniduff which of the English man
> Is cal'de Blacke water, and the Liffar deep,
> Sad Trowis, that once his people ouerran,
> Strong *Allo* tombling from Slewlogher steep,
> And *Mulla* mine, whose waues I whilom taught to
weep.

The other mention occurs in the former of the two
cantos *Of Mutability*. There the poet sings that the
place appointed for the trial of the titles and best
rights of both 'heavenly powers' and 'earthly wights'
was

> . . . vpon the highest hights
> Of *Arlo-hill* (Who knowes not *Arlo-hill?*)
> That is the highest head (in all mens sights)

Of my old father *Mole*, whom Shepheards quill
Renowmed hath with hymnes fit for a rurall skill.

   His poem called **Colin Clouts Come Home Again**,
written in 1591, and dedicated to Sir W. Raleigh 'from
my house at Kilcolman the 27 of December, 1591'{5}--
written therefore after a lengthy absence in England--
exhibits a full familiarity with the country round
about Kilcolman. On the whole then we may suppose that
his residence at Kilcolman began not later than 1588.
It was to be roughly and and terribly ended ten years
after.
   We may suppose he was living there in peace and
quiet, not perhaps undisturbed by growing murmurs of
discontent, by signs of unrepressed and irrepressible
hostility towards his nation, by ill-concealed
sympathies with the Spanish invaders amongst the native
population, when the Armada came and went.   The old
castle in which he had lived had been one of the
residences of the Earls of Desmond. It stood some two
miles from Doneraile, on the north side of a lake which
was fed by the river Awbeg or Mulla, as the poet
christened it.
   'Two miles north-west of Doneraile,' writes
Charles Smith in his Natural and Civil History of the
County and City of Cork, 1774, (i. 340, 341)--'is
Kilcoleman, a ruined castle of the Earls of Desmond,
but more celebrated for being the residence of the
immortal Spenser, when he composed his divine poem The
Faerie Queene. The castle is now almost level with
the ground, and was situated on the north side of a
fine lake, in the midst of a vast plain, terminated to
the east by the county of Waterford mountains; Bally-

howra hills to the north, or, as Spenser terms them,
the mountains of Mole, Nagle mountains to the south,
and the mountains of Kerry to the west. It commanded a
view of above half the breadth of Ireland; and must
have been, when the adjacent uplands were wooded, a
most pleasant and romantic situation; from whence, no
doubt, Spenser drew several parts of the scenery of his
poem.'

Here, then, as in some cool sequestered vale of
life, for some ten years, his visits to England
excepted, lived Spenser still singing sweetly, still,
as he might say, piping, with the woods answering him
and his echo ringing. Sitting in the shade he would
play many a 'pleasant fit;' he would sing

> Some hymne or morall laie,
> Or carol made to praise his loved lasse;

he would see in the rivers that flowed around his tower
beings who lived and loved, and would sing of their
mutual passions. It must have sounded strangely to
hear the notes of his sweet voice welling forth from
his old ruin--to hear music so subtle and refined
issuing from that scarred and broken relic of past
turbulencies --

> The shepheard swaines that did about him play
> . . . with greedie listfull eares
> Did stand astonisht at his curious skill
> Like hartlesse deare, dismayed with thunders sound.

He presents a picture such as would have delighted his
own fancy, though perhaps the actual experience may not

have been unalloyed with pain. It is a picture which
in many ways resembles that presented by one of kindred
type of genius, who has already been mentioned as of
affinity with him--by Wordsworth. Wordsworth too sang
in a certain sense from the shade, far away from the
vanity of courts, and the uproar of cities; sang 'from
a still place, remote from men;' sang, like his own
Highland girl, all alone with the 'vale profound'
'overflowing with the sound;' finding, too, objects of
friendship and love in the forms of nature which
surrounded his tranquil home.

Of these two poets in their various lonelinesses
one may perhaps quote those exquisite lines written by
one of them of a somewhat differently caused isolation:
each one of them too lacked

> Not friends for simple glee
> Nor yet for higher sympathy.
> To his side the fallow-deer
> Came and rested without fear;
> The eagle, lord of land and sea,
> Stooped down to pay him fealty.

.   .   .   .   .

> He knew the rocks which angels haunt
> Upon the mountains visitant;
> He hath kenned them taking wing;
> And into caves where Faeries sing
> He hath entered; and been told
> By voices how men lived of old.

Here now and then he was visited, it may be

supposed, by old friends. Perhaps that distinguished
son of the University of Cambridge, Gabriel Harvey, may
for a while have been his guest; he is introduced under
his pastoral name of Hobbinol, as present at the poet's
house on his return to Ireland. The most memorable of
these visits was that already alluded to--that paid to
him in 1589 by Sir Walter Raleigh, with whom it will be
remembered he had become acquainted some nine years
before. Raleigh, too, had received a grant from the
same huge forfeited estate, a fragment of which had
been given to Spenser. The granting of these, and
other shares of the Desmond estates, formed part of a
policy then vigorously entertained by the English
Government--the colonising of the so lately disordered
and still restless districts of Southern Ireland. The
recipients were termed 'undertakers;' it was one of
their duties to repair the ravages inflicted during the
recent tumults and bring the lands committed to them
into some state of cultivation and order.

The wars had been followed by a famine. 'Even in
the history of Ireland,' writes a recent biographer of
Sir Walter Raleigh, 'there are not many scenes more
full of horror that those which the historians of that
period rapidly sketch when showing us the condition of
almost the whole province of Munster in the year 1584,
and the years immediately succeeding.'{6}

The claims of his duties as an 'undertaker,' in
addition perhaps to certain troubles at court, where
his rival Essex was at this time somewhat superseding
him in the royal favour,{7} and making a temporary
absence not undesirable, brought Raleigh into Cork
County in 1589. A full account of this visit and its
important results is given us in Colin Clouts Come

Home Again, which gives us at the same time a charming
picture of the poet's life at Kilcolman. Colin
himself, lately returned home from England, tells his
brother shepherds, at their urgent request, of his
'passed fortunes.' He begins with Raleigh's visit.
One day, he tells them, as he sat

> Under the foote of Mole, that mountaine hore,
> Keeping my sheepe amongst the cooly shade
> Of the greene alders by the Mullaes shore,

a strange shepherd, who styled himself the Shepherd of
the Ocean --

> Whether allured with my pipes delight,
> Whose pleasing sound yshrilled far about,
> Or thither led by chaunce, I know not right --

found him out, and

> Provoked me to plaie some pleasant fit.

He sang, he tells us, a song of Mulla old father Mole's
daughter, and of another river called Bregog who loved
her. Then his guest sang in turn:--

> His song was all a lamentable lay
> Of great unkindnesse and of usage hard,
> Of Cynthia the ladie of the sea,
> Which from her presence faultlesse him debard,
> And ever and anon, with singults rife,
> He cryed out, to make his undersong:
> Ah! my loves queene and goddesse of my life,

Who shall me pittie when thou doest me wrong?

After they had made an end of singing, the shepherd of the ocean

> Gan to cast great lyking to my lore,
> And great dislyking to my lucklesse lot
> That banisht had my selfe, like wight forlore,
> Into that waste where I was quite forgot,

and presently persuaded him to accompany him 'his Cinthia to see.'

It has been seen from one of Harvey's letters that the ***Faerie Queene*** was already begun in 1580; and from what Bryskett says, and what Spenser says himself in his sonnets to Lord Grey, and to Lord Ormond, that it was proceeded with after the poet had passed over to Ireland. By the close of the year 1589 at least three books were completely finished. Probably enough parts of other books had been written; but only three were entirely ready for publication. No doubt part of the conversation that passed between Spenser and Raleigh related to Spenser's work. It may be believed that what was finished was submitted to Raleigh's judgment, and certainly concluded that it elicited his warmest approval.{8} One great object that Spenser proposed to himself when he assented to Raleigh's persuasion to visit England, was the publication of the first three books of his ***Faerie Queene***.

Notes

{1} One might quote of these poets, and those of a like
    spirit, Wordsworth's lines on 'the Characteristics
    of a Child three years old,' for in the respect
    therein mentioned, as in others, these poets are
    'as little children:'

    As a faggot sparkles on the hearth,
    Not less if unattended and alone,
    Than when both young and old sit gathered round,
    And take delight in its activity;
    Even so this happy creature of herself
    Is all-sufficient; Solitude to her
    Is blithe society, who fills the air
    With gladness and involuntary songs.

{2} See **Colin Clouts Come Home Again**, vv. 180-184,
    quoted below.
{3} This is the 'Lodovick' mentioned in Sonnet 33,
    quoted below. It was from him a little later, in
    1588, that Spenser obtained by 'purchase' the
    succession to the office of the Clerk of the
    Government Council of Munster. **See** Dr. Grosart's
    vol. i. p. 151.
{4} Dr. Birch refers in his note to The Ancient and
    Present State of the County and City of Cork, by
    Charles Smith, vol. i. book i. c. i. p. 58-63.
    Edit. Dublin 1750, 8vo. And Fiennes Moryson's
    Itinerary, part ii. p. 4.
{5} Todd proposes to regard this date as a printer's

error for 1595, quite unnecessarily.

{6} Mr. Edward Edwards, 1868, I. c. vi.; see also
    Colin Clouts Come Home Again, vv. 312-319.

{7} 'My lord of Essex hath chased Mr. Raleigh from the
    court and confined him in Ireland.'--Letter, dated
    August 17, 1589, from Captain Francis Allen to
    Antony Bacon, Esq.--Quoted by Todd from Dr. Birch's
    Memoirs of Queen Elizabeth.--See Mr. Edwards's
    Life of Raleigh, I. c. viii.

{8} See Raleigh's lines entitled 'A Vision upon this
    Conceipt of the ***Faery Queene***,' prefixed to the
    Faerie Queene.

CHAPTER III.

1590.

Thus after an absence of about nine years, Spenser
returned for a time to England; he returned 'bringing
his sheaves with him.' Whatever shadow of
misunderstanding had previously come between his
introducer--or perhaps re-introducer--and her Majesty
seems to have been speedily dissipated. Raleigh
presented him to the Queen, who, it would appear,
quickly recognised his merits. 'That goddess'

> To mine oaten pipe enclin'd her eare

That she thenceforth therein gan take delight,
And it desir'd at timely houres to heare
Al were my notes but rude and roughly dight.

In the Registers of the Stationers' Company for
1589 occurs to following entry, quoted here from Mr.
Arber's invaluable edition of them:--

Primo Die Decembris.--Master Ponsonbye.
Entered for his Copye a book intituled the fayre
Queene, dyposed into xii bookes &c. Aucthorysed
vnder thandes of the Archb. of Canterbery & bothe
the Wardens, vjd.

The letter of the author's prefixed to his poem
'expounding his whole intention in the course of this
worke, which for that it giveth great light to the
reader, for the better understanding is hereunto
annexed,' addressed to 'Sir Walter Raleigh, Knight,
Lord Wardein of the Stanneryes and her Maiesties
lieftenaunt in the county of Cornewayll,' is dated
January 23, 1589--that is, 1590, according to the New
Style. Shortly afterwards, in 1590, according to both
Old and New Styles, was published by William Ponsonby
'THE FAERIE QUEENE, Disposed into twelve books,
Fashioning XII Morall vertues.' That day, which we
spoke of as beginning to arise in 1579, now fully
dawned. The silence of well nigh two centuries was now
broken, not again to prevail, by mighty voices. During
Spenser's absence in Ireland, William Shakspere had
come up from the country to London. The exact date of
his advent it seems impossible to ascertain. Probably
enough it was 1585; but it may have been a little

later. We may, however, be fairly sure that by the
time of Spenser's arrival in London in 1589, Shakspere
was already occupying a notable position in his
profession as an actor; and what is more important,
there can be little doubt he was already known not only
as an actor, but as a play-writer. What he had already
written was not comparable with what he was to write
subsequently; but even those early dramas gave promise
of splendid fruits to be thereafter yielded. In 1593
appeared **Venus and Adonis**; in the following year
Lucrece; in 1595, Spenser's **Epithalamion**; in 1596,
the second three books of the **Faerie Queene**; in 1597
Romeo and Juliet, **King Richard the Second**, and
King Richard the Third were printed, and also Bacon's
Essays and the first part of Hooker's Ecclesiastical
Polity. During all these years various plays, of
increasing power and beauty, were proceeding from
Shakspere's hands; by 1598 about half of his extant
plays had certainly been composed. Early in 1599, he,
who may be said to have ushered in this illustrious
period, he whose radiance first dispersed the darkness
and made the day begin to be, our poet Spenser, died.
But the day did not die with him; it was then but
approaching its noon, when he, one of its brightest
suns, set. This day may be said to have fully broken
in the year 1590, when the first instalment of the
great work of Spenser's life made its appearance.

The three books were dedicated to the Queen. They
were followed in the original edition--are preceded in
later editions--first, by the letter to Raleigh above
mentioned; then by six poetical pieces of a
commendatory sort, written by friends of the poet--by
Raleigh who writes two of the pieces, by Harvey who now

praises and well-wishes the poem he had discountenanced some years before, by 'R.S.,' by 'H.B.,' by 'W.L.;' lastly, by seventeen sonnets addressed by the poet to various illustrious personages; to Sir Christopher Hatton, to Lord Burghley, to the Earl of Essex, Lord Charles Howard, Lord Grey of Wilton, Lord Buckhurst, Sir Francis Walsingham, Sir John Norris, Knight, lord president of Munster, Sir Walter Raleigh, the Countess of Pembroke, and others. The excellence of the poem was at once generally perceived and acknowledged. Spenser had already, as we have seen, gained great applause by his ***Shepheardes Calendar***, published some ten years before the coming out of his greater work. During these ten years he had resided out of England, as has been seen; but it is not likely his reputation had been languishing during his absence. Webbe in his ***Discourse of English Poetrie***, 1586, had contended 'that Spenser may well wear the garlande, and step before the best of all English poets.' The ***Shepheardes Calendar*** had been reprinted in 1581 and in 1586; probably enough, other works of his had been circulating in manuscript; the hopes of the country had been directed towards him; he was known to be engaged in the composition of a great poem. No doubt he found himself famous when he reached England on the visit suggested by Raleigh; he found a most eager expectant audience; and when at last his ***Faerie Queene*** appeared, it was received with the utmost delight and admiration. He was spoken of in the same year with its appearance as the new laureate.{1} In the spring of the following year he received a pension from the crown of 50*l*. per annum. Probably, however, then, as in later days, the most ardent appreciators of of Spenser

were the men of the same craft with himself--the men
who too, though in a different degree, or in a
different kind, possessed the 'vision and the faculty
divine.'

This great estimation of the *Faerie Queene* was
due not only to the intrinsic charms of the poem--to
its exquisitely sweet melody, its intense pervading
sense of beauty, its abundant fancifulness, its subtle
spirituality--but also to the time of its appearance.
For then nearly two centuries no great poem had been
written in the English tongue. Chaucer had died
heirless. Occleve's lament over that great spirit's
decease had not been made without occasion:--

> Alas my worthie maister honorable
> This londis verray tresour and richesse
> Deth by thy dethe hathe harm irreperable
> Unto us done; hir vengeable duresse
> Dispoiled hathe this londe of swetnesse
> Of Rethoryk fro us; to Tullius
> Was never man so like amonges us.{2}

And the doleful confession this orphaned rhymer makes
for himself, might have been well made by all the men
of his age in England:--

> My dere mayster, God his soule quite,
> And fader Chaucer fayne would have me taught,
> But I was dull, and learned lyte or naught.

No worthy scholar had succeeded the great master. The
fifteenth century in England had abounded in movements
of profound social and political interest--in movements

which eventually fertilised and enriched and ripened
the mind of the nation; but, not unnaturally, the
immediate literary results had been of no great value.
In the reign of Henry VIII, the condition of
literature, for various reasons, had greatly improved.
Surrey and Wyatt had heralded the advent of a brighter
era. From their time the poetical succession had never
failed altogether. The most memorable name in our
literature between their time and the ***Faerie Queene***
is that of Sackville, Lord Buckhurst--a name of note in
the history of both our dramatic and non-dramatic
poetry. Sackville was capable of something more than
lyrical essays. He it was who designed the Mirror for
Magistrates. To that poem, important as compared with
the poetry of its day, for its more pretentious
conception, he himself contributed the two best pieces
that form part of it--the ***Induction*** and the
Complaint of Buckingham. These pieces are marked by
some beauties of the same sort as those which
especially characterise Spenser; but they are but
fragments; and in spirit they belong to an age which
happily passed away shortly after the accession of
Queen Elizabeth--they are penetrated by that despondent
tone which is so strikingly audible in our literature
in the middle years of the sixteeth century, not
surprisingly, if the general history of the time be
considered. Meanwhile, our language had changed much,
and Chaucer had grown almost unintelligible to the
ordinary reader. Therefore, about the year 1590, the
nation was practically without a great poem. At the
same time, it then, if ever, truly needed one. Its
power of appreciation had been quickened and refined by
the study of the poetries of other countries; it had

translated and perused the classical writers with enthusiasm; it had ardently pored over the poetical literature of Italy. Then its life had lately been ennobled by deeds of splendid courage crowned with as splendid success. In the year 1590, if ever, this country, in respect of its literary condition and in respect of its general high and noble excitement, was ready for the reception of a great poem.

Such a poem undoubtedly was the *Faerie Queene*, although it may perhaps be admitted that it was a work likely to win favour with the refined and cultured sections of the community rather than with the community at large. Strongly impressed on it as were the instant influences of the day, yet in many ways it was marked by a certain archaic character. It depicted a world--the world of chivalry and romance--which was departed; it drew its images, its forms of life, its scenery, its very language, from the past. Then the genius of our literature in the latter part of Queen Elizabeth's reign was emphatically dramatic; in the intense life of these years men longed for reality. Now the *Faerie Queene* is one long idealizing. These circumstances are to accounted for partly by the character of Spenser's genius, partly by the fact already stated that chronologically Spenser is the earliest of the great spirits of his day. In truth he stands between two worlds: he belongs partly to the new time, partly to the old; he is the last of one age, he is the first of another; he stretches out one hand into the past to Chaucer, the other rests upon the shoulder of Milton.

Notes

{1} Nash's **Supplication of Pierce Pennilesse**, 1592.
{2} Skeat's **Specimens of English Literature**, p. 14.

CHAPTER IV.

1591-1599.

It is easy to imagine how intensely Spenser enjoyed his
visit to London. It is uncertain to what extent that
visit was prolonged. He dates the dedication of his
Colin Clouts Come Home Again 'from my house at
Kilcolman, the 27 of December, 1591.' On the other
hand, the dedication of his **Daphnaida** is dated
'London this first of Januarie 1591,' that is 1592
according to our new style. Evidently there is some
mistake here. Prof. Craik 'suspects' that in the
latter instance 'the date January 1591' is used in the
modern meaning; he quotes nothing to justify such a
suspicion; but it would seem to be correct. Todd and
others have proposed to alter the '1591' in the former
instance to 1595, the year in which Colin Clouts Come
Home Again was published, and with which the allusions
made in the poem to contemporary writers agree; but

this proposal is, as we shall see, scarcely tenable.
The manner in which the publisher of the **Complaints**,
1591, of which publication we shall speak presently,
introduces that work to the 'gentle reader,' seems to
show that the poet was not at the time of the
publishing easily accessible. He speaks of having
endeavoured 'by all good meanes (for the better
encrease and accomplishment of your delights) to get
into my hands such small poems of the same authors, as
I heard were disperst abroad in sundrie hands, and not
easie to bee come by by himselfe; some of them having
been diverslie imbeziled and purloyned from him since
his departure ouer sea.' He says he understands
Spenser 'wrote sundrie others' besides those now
collected, 'besides some other Pamphlets looselie
scattered abroad . . . which when I can either by
himselfe or otherwise attaine too I meane likewise for
your fauour sake to set foorth.' It may be supposed
with much probability that Spenser returned to his
Irish castle some time in 1591, in all likelihood after
February, in which month he received the pension
mentioned above, and on the other hand so as to have
time to write the original draught of Colin Clouts
Come Home Again before the close of December.

The reception of the **Faerie Queene** had been so
favourable that in 1591--it would seem, as has been
shown, after Spenser's departure--the publisher of that
poem determined to put forth what other poems by the
same hand he could gather together. The result was a
volume entitled '**Complaints**, containing sundrie small
Poemes of the Worlds Vanitie, whereof the next page
maketh mention. By Ed. Sp.' 'The next page' contains
'a note of the Sundrie Poemes contained in this

volume:'

1. The Ruines of Time.
2. The Teares of the Muses.
3. Virgils Gnat.
4. Prosopopoia or Mother Hubbards Tale.
5. The Ruines of Rome, by Bellay.
6. Muiopotmos or The Tale of the Butterflie.
7. Visions of the Worlds Vanitie.
8. Bellayes Visions.
9. Petrarches Visions.

In a short notice addressed to the Gentle Reader which follows--the notice just referred to--the publisher of the volume mentions other works by Spenser, and promises to publish them too 'when he can attain to' them. These works are *Ecclesiastes*, The Seven Psalms, *and* Canticum Canticorum--these three no doubt translations of parts of the Old Testament--A Sennight Slumber, The State of Lovers, *the* Dying Pelican--doubtless the work mentioned, as has been seen, in one of Spenser's letters to Harvey--The Howers of the Lord, *and* The Sacrifice of a Sinner. Many of these works had probably been passing from hand to hand in manuscript for many years. That old method of circulation survived the invention of the printing press for many generations. The perils of it may be illustrated from the fate of the works just mentioned. It would seem that the publisher never did attain to them; and they have all perished. With regard to the works which were printed and preserved, the Ruines of Time, as the Dedication shows, was written during Spenser's memorable visit of 1589-91 to England. It is

in fact an elegy dedicated to the Countess of Pembroke,
on the death of Sir Philip Sidney, 'that most brave
Knight, your most noble brother deceased.' 'Sithens my
late cumming into England,' the poet writes in the
Epistle Dedicatorie, 'some friends of mine (which might
much prevaile with me and indeede commaund me) knowing
with howe straight bandes of duetie I was tied to him;
as also bound unto that noble house (of which the
chiefe hope then rested in him) have sought to revive
them by upbraiding me; for that I have not shewed anie
thankefull remembrance towards him or any of them; but
suffer their names to sleepe in silence and
forgetfulnesse. Whome chieflie to satisfie, or els to
avoide that fowle blot of unthankefulnesse, I have
conceived this small Poeme, intituled by a generall
name of the **Worlds Ruines**: yet speciallie intended to
the renowming of that noble race from which both you
and he sprong, and to the eternizing of some of the
chiefe of them late deceased.' This poem is written in
a tone that had been extremely frequent during
Spenser's youth. Its text is that ancient one 'Vanity
of Vanities; all is Vanity'--a very obvious text in all
ages, but perhaps especially so, as has been hinted, in
the sixteenth century, and one very frequently adopted
at that time. This text is treated in a manner
characteristic of the age. It is exemplified by a
series of visions. The poet represents himself as
seeing at Verulam an apparition of a woman weeping over
the decay of that ancient town. This woman stands for
the town itself. Of its whilome glories, she says,
after a vain recounting of them,

They all are gone and with them is gone,

Ne ought to me remaines, but to lament
My long decay.

No one, she continues, weeps with her, no one remembers
her,

Save one that maugre fortunes injurie
And times decay, and enuies cruell tort
Hath writ my record in true seeming sort.

Cambden the nourice of antiquitie,
And lanterne unto late succeeding age,
To see the light of simple veritie
Buried in ruines, through the great outrage
Of her owne people, led with warlike rage,
Cambden, though time all moniments obscure,
Yet thy just labours ever shall endure.

Then she rebukes herself for these selfish moanings by
calling to mind how far from solitary she is in her
desolation. She recalls to mind the great ones of the
land who have lately fallen--Leicester, and Warwick,
and Sidney--and wonders no longer at her own ruin. Is
not *Transit Gloria* the lesson taught everywhere?
Then other visions and emblems of instability are seen,
some of them not darkly suggesting that what passes
away from earth and apparently ends may perhaps be
glorified elsewhere. The second of these collected
poems--*The Teares of the Muses*--dedicated, as we have
seen, to one of the poet's fair cousins, the Lady
Strange, deplores the general intellectual condition of
the time. It is doubtful whether Spenser fully
conceived what a brilliant literary age was beginning

about the year 1590. Perhaps his long absence in
Ireland, the death of Sidney who was the great hope of
England Spenser knew, the ecclesiastical controversies
raging when he revisited England, may partly account
for his despondent tone with reference to literature.
He introduces each Muse weeping for the neglect and
contempt suffered by her respective province. He who
describes these tears was himself destined to dry them;
and Shakspere, who, if anyone, was to make the faces of
the Muses blithe and bright, was now rapidly
approaching his prime. There can be little doubt that
at a later time Spenser was acquainted with Shakspere;
for Spenser was an intimate friend of the Earl of
Essex; Shakspere was an intimate friend of the Earl of
Southampton, who was one of the most attached friends
of that Earl of Essex. And a personal acquaintance
with Shakspere may have been one of the most memorable
events of Spenser's visit to London in 1589. We would
gladly think that Thalia in the *Teares of the Muses*
refers in the following passage to Shakspere: the comic
stage, she says, is degraded,

> And he the man whom Nature selfe had made
> To mock herselfe and Truth to imitate,
> With kindly counter under Mimick shade,
> Our pleasant Willy, ah! is dead of late;
> With whom all joy and jolly meriment
> Is also deaded and in dolour drent.

The context shows that by 'dead' is not meant physical
death, but that

> That same gentle spirit, from whose pen

Large streames of honnie and sweete nectar flowe,

produces nothing, sits idle-handed and silent, rather than pander to the grosser tastes of the day. But this view, attractive as it is, can perhaps hardly be maintained. Though the *Teares of the Muses* was not published, as we have seen, till 1591, it was probably written some years earlier, and so before the star of Shakspere had arisen. Possibly by Willy is meant Sir Philip Sidney, a favourite haunt of whose was his sister's house at Wilton on the river Wiley or Willey, and who had exhibited some comic power in his masque, *The Lady of May*, acted before the Queen in 1578. Some scholars, however, take 'Willy' to denote John Lily. Thus the passage at present remains dark. If written in 1590, it certainly cannot mean Sidney, who had been dead some years; just possibly, but not probably, it might in that case mean Shakspere.

Of the remaining works published in his *Complaints*, the only other one of recent composition is *Muiopotmos*, which, as Prof. Craik suggests, would seem to be an allegorical narrative of some matter recently transpired. It is dated 1590, but nothing is known of any earlier edition than that which appears in the *Complaints*. Of the other pieces by far the most interesting is *Prosopopoia, or Mother Hubbards Tale*, not only because it is in it, as has been said, Spenser most carefully, though far from successfully, imitates his great master Chaucer, but for its intrinsic merit-- for its easy style, its various incidents, its social pictures. In the dedication he speaks of it as 'These my idle labours; which having long sithens composed in the raw conceipt of my youth, I lately amongst other papers lighted upon, and was by others, which liked the same, mooved to set them foorth.' However long before its publication the poem in the main was written, possibly some additions were made to it in or about the year 1590; as for instance, the well-known passage describing 'a suitor's state,' which reflects too clearly a bitter personal experience to have been composed before Spenser had grown so familiar with the Court as he became during his visit to England under Raleigh's patronage. But it is conceivable that his experiences in 1578 and 1579 inspired the lines in question.

The remaining pieces in the *Complaints* consist of translations or imitations, composed probably some years before, though probably in some cases, as has been shown, revised or altogether recast.

Probably in the same year with the *Complaints*-- that is in 1591--was published *Daphnaida*,{1} 'an Elegie upon the death of the noble and vertuous Douglas Howard, daughter and heire of Henry Lord Howard, Viscount Byndon, and wife of Arthur Georges, Esquire.' This elegy was no doubt written before Spenser returned to Ireland. It is marked by his characteristic diffuseness, abundance, melody.

Certainly before the close of the year 1591 Spenser found himself once more in his old castle of Kilcolman. A life at Court could never have suited him, however irksome at times his isolation in Ireland may have seemed. When his friends wondered at his returning unto

       This barrein soyle,
Where cold and care and penury do dwell,

Here to keep sheepe with hunger and with toyle,

he made the answer that he,

> Whose former dayes
> Had in rude fields bene altogether spent,
> Durst not adventure such unknowen wayes,
> Nor trust the guile of fortunes blandishment;
> But rather chose back to my sheepe to tourne,
> Whose utmost hardnesse I before had tryde,
> Then, having learnd repentance late, to mourne
> Emongst those wretches which I there descryde.

That life, with all its intrigues and self-seekings and scandals, had no charms for him. Once more settled in his home, he wrote an account of his recent absence from it, which he entitled Colin Clouts Come Home Again. This poem was not published till 1595; but, whatever additions were subsequently made to it, there can be no doubt it was originally written immediately after his return to Ireland. Sitting in the quiet to which he was but now restored, he reviewed the splendid scenes he had lately witnessed; he recounted the famous wits he had met, and the fair ladies he had seen in the great London world; and dedicated this exquisite diary to the friend who had introduced him into that brilliant circle. It would seem that Raleigh had accused him of indolence. That ever-restless schemer could not appreciate the poet's dreaminess. 'That you may see,' writes Spenser, 'that I am not alwaies ydle as yee think, though not greatly well occupied, nor altogither undutifull, though not precisely officious, I make you present of this simple pastorall, unworthie

of your higher conceipt for the meanesse of the stile,
but agreeing with the truth in circumstance and matter.
The which I humbly beseech you to accept in part of
paiment of the infinite debt in which I acknowledge
myselfe bounden unto you for your singular favours and
sundrie good turnes shewed to me at my late being in
England, &c.'

The conclusion of this poem commemorates, as we
have seen, Spenser's enduring affection for that
Rosalind who so many years before had turned away her
ears from his suit. It must have been some twelve
months after those lines were penned, that the writer
conceived an ardent attachment for one Elizabeth. The
active research of Dr. Grosart has discovered that this
lady belonged to the Boyle family--a family already of
importance and destined to be famous. The family seat
was at Kilcoran, near Youghal, and so we understand
Spenser's singing of 'The sea that neighbours to her
near.' Thus she lived in the same county with her
poet. The whole course of the wooing and the winning
is portrayed in the *Amoretti or Sonnets* and the
Epithalamium. It may be gathered from these
biographically and otherwise interesting pieces, that
it was at the close of the year 1592 that the poet was
made a captive of that beauty he so fondly describes.
The first three sonnets would seem to have been written
in that year. The fourth celebrates the beginning of
the year 1593--the beginning according to our modern
way of reckoning. All through that year 1593 the lover
sighed, beseeched, adored, despaired, prayed again.
Fifty-eight sonnets chronicle the various hopes and
fears of that year. The object of his passion remained
as steel and flint, while he wept and wailed and

pleaded. His life was a long torment.

> In vaine I seeke and sew to her for grace
>   And doe myne humbled hart before her poure;
> The whiles her foot she in my necke doth place
>   And tread my life downe in the lowly floure.

In Lent she is his 'sweet saynt,' and he vows to find some fit service for her.

> Her temple fayre is built within my mind
> In which her glorious image placed is.

But all his devotion profited nothing, and he thinks it were better 'at once to die.' He marvels at her cruelty. He cannot address himself to further composition of his great poem. The accomplishment of that great work were

> Sufficient werke for one man's simple head,
> All were it, as the rest, but rudely writ.
> How then should I, without another wit,
> Thinck ever to endure so tedious toyle?
> Sith that this one is tost with troublous fit
> Of a proud love that doth my spirit spoyle.

He falls ill in his body too. When the anniversary of his being carried into captivity comes round, he declares, as has already been quoted, that the year just elapsed has appeared longer than all the forty years of his life that had preceded it (sonnet 60). In the beginning of the year 1594,

> After long stormes and tempests sad assay
> Which hardly I endured hertofore
> In dread of death and daungerous dismay
> With which my silly bark was tossed sore,

he did 'at length descry the happy shore.' The heart
of his mistress softened towards him. The last twenty-
five sonnets are for the most part the songs of a lover
accepted and happy. It would seem that by this time he
had completed three more books of the **Faerie Queene**,
and he asks leave in sonnet 70,

>   In pleasant mew
> To sport my Muse and sing my loves sweet praise,
> The contemplation of whose heavenly hew
> My spirit to an higher pitch doth raise.

Probably the Sixth Book was concluded in the first part
of the year 1594, just after his long wooing had been
crowned with success. In the tenth canto of that book
he introduces the lady of his love, and himself
'piping' unto her. In a rarely pleasant place on a
fair wooded hill-top Calidore sees the Graces dancing,
and Colin Clout piping merrily. With these goddesses
is a fourth maid; it is to her alone that Colin
pipes:--

> Pype, jolly shepheard, pype thou now apace
> Unto thy love that made thee low to lout;
> Thy love is present there with thee in place;
> Thy love is there advaunst to be another Grace.

Of this fourth maid the poet, after sweetly praising

the daughters of sky-ruling Jove, sings in this wise:--

Who can aread what creature mote she bee;
Whether a creature or a goddesse graced
With heavenly gifts from heven first enraced?
But what so sure she was, she worthy was
To be the fourth with those three other placed,
Yet she was certes but a countrey lasse;
Yet she all other countrey lasses farre did passe.

So farre, as doth the daughter of the day
All other lesser lights in light excell;
So farre doth she in beautyfull array
Above all other lasses beare the bell;
Ne lesse in vertue that beseems her well
Doth she exceede the rest of all her race.

The phrase 'country lass' in this rapturous passage has been taken to signify that she to whom it applied was of mean origin; but it scarcely bears this construction. Probably all that is meant is that her family was not connected with the Court or the Court circle. She was not high-born; but she was not low-born. The final sonnets refer to some malicious reports circulating about him, and to some local separation between the sonneteer and his mistress. This separation was certainly ended in the June following his acceptance--that is, the June of 1594; for in that month, on St. Barnabas' day, that is, on the 11th, Spenser was married. This event Spenser celebrates in the finest, the most perfect of all his poems, in the most beautiful of all bridal songs--in his *Epithalamion*. He had many a time sung for others; he now bade the Muses crown their heads with garlands and help him his own love's praises to resound:--

> So I unto my selfe alone will sing,
> The woods shall to me answer, and my echo ring.

Then, with the sweetest melody and a refinement and grace incomparable, he sings with a most happy heart of various matters of the marriage day--of his love's waking, of the merry music of the minstrels, of her coming forth in all the pride of her visible loveliness, of that 'inward beauty of her lively spright' which no eyes can see, of her standing before the altar, her sad eyes still fastened on the ground, of the bringing her home, of the rising of the evening star, and the fair face of the moon looking down on his bliss not unfavourably, as he would hope. The *Amoretti* and *Epithalamion* were registered at the Stationers' Hall on the 19th of November following the marriage. They were published in 1595, Spenser--as appears from the 'Dedication' of them to Sir Robert Needham, written by the printer Ponsonby--being still absent from England.

Meanwhile the poet had been vexed by other troubles besides those of a slowly requited passion. Mr. Hardiman,{2} in his *Irish Minstrelsy*, has published three petitions presented in 1593 to the Lord Chancellor of Ireland by Maurice, Lord Roche, Viscount Fermoy, two against 'one Edmond Spenser, gentleman', one against one Joan Ny Callaghan--who is said to act 'by supportation and maintenance of Edmond Spenser, gentleman, a heavy adversary to your suppliant.'

'Where,' runs the first petition, 'one Edmond Spenser, gentleman, hath lately exhibited suit against your suppliant for three ploughlands, parcels of Shanballymore (your suppliant's inheritance) before the Vice-President and Council of Munster, which land hath been heretofore decreed for your suppliant against the said Spenser and others under whom he conveyed; and nevertheless for that the said Spenser, being Clerk of the Council in the said province, and did assign his office unto one Nicholas Curteys among other agreements with covenant that during his life he should be free in the said office for his causes, by occasion of which immunity he doth multiply suits against your suppliant in the said province upon pretended title of others &c.' The third petition averred that 'Edmond Spenser of Kilcolman, gentleman, hath entered into three ploughlands, parcel of Ballingerath, and disseised your suppliant thereof, and continueth by countenance and greatness the possession thereof, and maketh great waste of the wood of the said land, and converteth a great deal of corn growing thereupon to his proper use, to the damage of the complainant of two hundred pounds sterling. Whereunto,' continues the document, which is preserved in the Original Rolls Office, 'the said Edmond Spenser appearing in person had several days prefixed unto him peremptorily to answer, which he neglected to do.' Therefore 'after a day of grace given,' on the 12th of February, 1594, Lord Roche was decreed the possession. Perhaps the absence from his lady love referred to in the concluding sonnets was occasioned by this litigation. Perhaps also the 'false forged lyes'--the malicious reports circulated about him--referred to in Sonnet 85, may have been connected with these appeals against him. It is clear that all his dreams of Faerie did not make him neglectful of his earthly estate. Like Shakspere, like Scott, Spenser did not cease to be a man of the world--we use the phrase in no unkindly sense--because he was a poet. He was no mere visionary, helpless in the ordinary affairs of life. In the present case it would appear that he was even too keen in looking after his own interests. Professor Craik charitably suggests that his poverty 'rather than rapacity may be supposed to have urged whatever of hardness there was in his proceedings.' It is credible enough that these proceedings made him highly unpopular with the native inhabitants of the district, and that they were not forgotten when the day of reckoning came. 'His name,' says Mr. Hardiman, on the authority of *Trotter's Walks in Ireland*,{3} 'is still remembered in the vicinity of Kilcolman; but the people entertain no sentiments of respect or affection for his memory.'

In the same year with the *Amoretti* was published *Colin Clouts Come Home Again*, several additions having been made to the original version.

Probably at the close of this year 1595 Spenser a second time crossed to England, accompanied, it may be supposed, by his wife, carrying with him in manuscript the second three books of his *Faerie Queene*, which, as we have seen, were completed before his marriage, and also a prose work, A View of the Present State of Ireland. Mr. Collier quotes the following entry from the Stationers' Register:--

20 die Januarii [1595].--Mr. Ponsonby. Entred &c. The Second Part of the Faerie Queene, cont.

the 4, 5, and 6 bookes, vj***d***.

This second instalment--which was to be the last--of his great poem was duly published in that year. The ***View of the Present State of Ireland*** was not registered till April 1598, and then only conditionally. It was not actually printed till 1633. During his stay in England he wrote the Hymns to Heavenly Love and Heavenly Beauty, and the ***Prothalamion***, which were to be his last works.

More than four years had elapsed since Spenser had last visited London. During that period certain memorable works had been produced; the intellectual power of that day had expressed itself in no mean manner. When he arrived in London towards the close of the year 1595, he would find Shakspere splendidly fulfilling the promise of his earlier days; he would find Ben Jonson just becoming known to fame; he would find Bacon already drawing to him the eyes of his time. Spenser probably spent the whole of the year 1596, and part of 1597, in England. In 1597 appeared, as has already been said, the first part of Hooker's ***Ecclesiastical Polity***, and Bacon's ***Essays***, and also Jonson's ***Every Man in His Own Humour***.

The reigning favourite at this time was the Earl of Essex. In 1596 his successful descent upon Cadiz raised him to the zenith of his fame. With this nobleman Spenser was on terms of intimacy. At his London house in the Strand--a house which had previously been inhabited by Spenser's earlier patron, the Earl of Leicester--it stood where Essex Street now is, and is still represented by the two pillars which stand at the bottom of that street--Spenser no doubt

renewed his friendship with Shakspere. This intimacy
with Essex, with whatever intellectual advantages it
may have been attended, with whatever bright spirits it
may have brought Spenser acquainted, probably impeded
his prospects of preferment. There can be no doubt
that one of the motives that brought him to England was
a desire to advance his fortunes. Camden describes him
as always poor. His distaste for his residence in
Ireland could not but have been aggravated by his
recent legal defeat. But he looked in vain for further
preferment. He had fame, and to spare, and this was to
suffice. It was during this sojourn in England that he
spoke of himself, as we have seen, as one

>   Whom sullein care
> Through discontent of my long fruitlesse stay
> In Princes court and expectation vayne
> Of idle hopes which still doe fly away
> Like empty shaddows, did afflict my brayne.

The publication of the second three books of the
Faerie Queene, with a re-impression of the first
three books, placed him on the highest pinnacle of
fame. Its plentiful references to passing events--its
adumbrations of the history of the time--however it
might damage the permanent value of the work from an
artistic point of view, increased its immediate
popularity. How keenly these references were
appreciated appears from the anxiety of the Scotch King
to have the poet prosecuted for his picture of Duessa,
in whom Mary Queen of Scots was generally recognised.
'Robert Bowes, the English ambassador in Scotland,
writing to Lord Burghley from Edinburgh 12th November,

1596, states that great offence was conceived by the
King against Edmund Spenser for publishing in print, in
the second part of the *Faery Queen*, ch. 9, some
dishonourable effects, as the King deemed, against
himself and his mother deceased. Mr. Bowes states that
he had satisfied the King as to the privilege under
which the book was published, yet he still desired that
Edmund Spenser for this fault might be tried and
punished. It further appears, from a letter from
George Nicolson to Sir Robert Cecil, dated Edinburgh,
25 February, 1597-8, that Walter Quin, an Irishman, was
answering Spenser's book, whereat the King was
offended.'{4}

   The *View of the Present State of Ireland*,
written dialogue-wise between Eudoxus and Iren{ae}us,
though not printed, as has been said, till 1633, seems
to have enjoyed a considerable circulation in a
manuscript form. There are manuscript copies of this
tractate at Cambridge, at Dublin, at Lambeth, and in
the British Museum. It is partly antiquarian, partly
descriptive, partly political. It exhibits a profound
sense of the unsatisfactory state of the country--a
sense which was presently to be justified in a
frightful manner. Spenser had not been deaf to the
ever-growing murmurs of discontent by which he and his
countrymen had been surrounded. He was not in advance
of his time in the policy he advocates for the
administration of Ireland. He was far from
anticipating that policy of conciliation whose
triumphant application it may perhaps be the signal
honour of our own day to achieve. The measures he
proposes are all of a vigorously repressive kind; they
are such measures as belong to a military occupancy,

not to a statesmanly administration. He urges the stationing numerous garrisons; he is for the abolishing native customs. Such proposals won a not unfavourable hearing at that time. They have been admired many a time since.

It is to this work of Spenser's that Protector Cromwell alludes in a letter to his council in Ireland, in favour of William Spenser, grandson of Edmund Spenser, from whom an estate of lands in the barony of Fermoy, in the county of Cork, descended on him. 'His grandfather,' he writes, 'was that Spenser who, by his writings touching the reduction of the Irish to civility, brought on him the odium of that nation; and for those works and his other good services Queen Elizabeth conferred on him that estate which the said William Spenser now claims.'{5} This latter statement is evidently inaccurate. Spenser, as we have seen, had already held his estate for some years when he brought his *View* to England.

Spenser dates the dedication of his *Hymns* from Greenwich, September 1, 1596. Of these four hymns, two had been in circulation for some years, though now for the first time printed; the other two now first appeared. 'Having in the greener times of my youth,' he writes, 'composed these former two hymnes in the praise of love and beautie, and finding that the same too much pleased those of like age and disposition, which being too vehemently caried with that kind of affection, do rather sucke out poyson to their strong passion than hony to their honest delight, I was moved by one of you two most excellent ladies [the ladies Margaret, Countess of Cumberland, Mary, Countess of Warwick] to call in the same; but unable so to doe, by reason that many copies thereof were formerly scattered abroad, I resolved at least to amend, and by way of retraction to reforme them, making (instead of those two hymnes of earthly or naturall love and beautie) two others of heavenly and celestiall.' This passage is interesting for the illustration it provides of Spenser's popularity. It is also highly interesting, if the poems themselves be read in the light of it, as showing the sensitive purity of the poet's nature. It is difficult to conceive how those 'former hymns' should in any moral respect need amending. The moralising and corrective purpose with which the two latter were written perhaps diminished their poetical beauty; but the themes they celebrate are such as Spenser could not but ever descant upon with delight; they were such as were entirely congenial to his spirit. He here set forth special teachings of his great master Plato, and abandoned himself to the high spiritual contemplations he loved. But perhaps the finest of these four hymns is the second--that in honour of Beauty. Beauty was indeed the one worship of Spenser's life--not mere material beauty--not 'the goodly hew of white and red with which the cheekes are sprinkled,' or 'the sweete rosy leaves so fairly spred upon the lips,' or 'that golden wyre,' or 'those sparckling stars so bright,' but that inner spiritual beauty, of which fair hair and bright eyes are but external expressions.

> So every spirit, as it is most pure
> And hath in it the more of heavenly light,
> So it the fairer bodie doth procure
> To habit in, and it more fairely dight

With chearfull grace and amiable sight;
For of the soule the bodie forme doth take,
For soule is forme and doth the bodie make.

This hymn is one of high refined rapture.

Before the close of the year 1596 Spenser wrote
and published the ***Prothalamion*** or 'A spousall verse
made in honour of the double marriage of the two
honourable and vertuous ladies, the ladie Elizabeth,
and the ladie Katherine Somerset, daughters to the
right honourable the Earle of Worcester, and espoused
to the two worthie gentlemen, M. Henry Gilford and M.
William Peter Esquyers.' It was composed after the
return of Essex from Spain, for he is introduced in the
poem as then residing at his house in the Strand. It
is a poem full of grace and beauty, and of matchless
melodiousness.

This is the last complete poem Spenser wrote. No
doubt he entertained the idea of completing his Faerie
Queene; and perhaps it was after 1596 that he composed
the two additional cantos, which are all, so far as is
known, that he actually wrote. But the last poem
completed and published in his lifetime was the
Prothalamion.

This second visit to England at last came to an
end. It was probably in 1597 that he returned once
more to Kilcolman. In the following year he was
recommended by her Majesty for Sheriff of Cork. But
his residence in Ireland was now to be rudely
terminated.

The Irishry had, ever since the suppression of
Desmond's rebellion in 1582, been but waiting for
another opportunity to rise, that suppression not

having brought pacification in its train. In the autumn of 1598 broke out another of these fearful insurrections, of which the history of English rule in Ireland is mainly composed.

In the September of that year Spenser was at the zenith of his prosperity. In that month arrived the letter recommending his appointment to be Sheriff of Cork. It seems legitimate to connect this mark of royal favour with the fact that at the beginning of the preceding month Lord Burghley had deceased. The great obstructor of the Queen's bounty was removed, and Spenser might hope that now, at last, the hour of his prosperity was come. So far as is known, his domestic life was serene and happy. The joys of the husband had been crowned with those of the father. Two sons, as may be gathered from the names given to them--they were christened Sylvanus and Peregrine--had been by this time born to him; according to Sir William Betham, who drew up a pedigree of Spenser's family, another son and a daughter had been born between the birth of Sylvanus and that of Peregrine. Then he was at this time the recognised prince of living poets. The early autumn of 1598 saw him in the culminating enjoyment of all these happinesses.

In October the insurgents burst roughly in upon his peace. No doubt his occupation of the old castle of Desmond had ever been regarded with fierce jealousy. While he had dreamed his dreams and sung his songs in the valley, there had been curses muttered against him from the hills around. At last the day of vengeance came. The outraged natives rushed down upon Kilcolman; the poet and his family barely made their escape; his home was plundered and burned. According to Ben

Jonson, in the conversation with Drummond, quoted
above, not all his family escaped; one little child,
new born, perished in the flames. But, indeed, the
fearfulness of this event needs no exaggeration. In
profound distress Spenser arrived once more in London,
bearing a despatch from Sir Thomas Norreys, President
of Munster, to the Secretary of State, and of course
himself full of direct and precise information as to
the Irish tumult, having also drawn up an address to
the Queen on the subject. Probably, the hardships and
horrors he had undergone completely prostrated him. On
January 16, 1599, he died in Westminster. As to the
exact place, a manuscript note found by Brand, the
well-known antiquary, on the title-page of a copy of
the second edition of the *Faerie Queene*, though not
of indisputable value, may probably enough be accepted,
and it names King Street. Ben Jonson says, 'he died
for lack of bread;' but this must certainly be an
exaggeration. No doubt he returned to England
'inops'--in a state of poverty--as Camden says; but it
is impossible to believe that he died of starvation.
His friend Essex and many another were ready to
minister to his necessities if he needed their
ministry. Jonson's story is that he 'refused twenty
pieces sent him by my lord Essex, and said he was sure
he had no time to spend them.' This story, if it is
anything more than a mere vulgar rumour, so far as it
shows anything, shows that he was in no such very
extreme need of succour. Had his destitution been so
complete, he would have accepted the pieces for his
family, even though 'he had no time to spend them
himself.' It must be remembered that he was still in
receipt of a pension from the crown; a pension of no

very considerable amount, perhaps, but still large enough to satisfy the pangs of hunger. But numerous passages might be quoted to show that he died in somewhat straitened circumstances.

It was said, some thirty-four years after Spenser's death, that in his hurried flight from Ireland the remaining six books of the **Faerie Queene** were lost. But it is very unlikely that those books were ever completed.{6} Perhaps some fragments of them may have perished in the flames at Kilcolman--certainly only two cantos have reached us. These were first printed in 1611, when the first six books were republished. The general testimony of his contemporaries is that his song was broken off in the midst. Says Browne in his **Britannia's Pastorals** (Book ii. s. 1):--

> But ere he ended his melodious song,
> An host of angels flew the cloud among,
> And rapt this swan from his attentive mates
> To make him one of their associates
> In heaven's faire choir.

One S. A. Cokain writes:--

> If, honour'd Colin, thou hadst lived so long
> As to have finished thy Fairy song,
> Not only mine but all tongues would confess,
> Thou hadst exceeded old M{ae}onides.

He was buried near Chaucer--by his own wish, it is said--in Westminster Abbey, 'poetis funus ducentibus,' with poets following him to the grave--bearing the pall, as we might say--the Earl of Essex furnishing the funeral expenses, according to Camden. It would seem from a passage in Browne's ***Britannia's Pastorals*** 'that the Queen ordered a monument to be erected over him, but that the money was otherwise appropriated by one of her agents.' The present monument, restored in 1778, was erected by Anne, Countess of Dorset, in 1620.

His widow married again before 1603, as we learn from a petition presented to the Lord Chancellor of Ireland in that year, in which Sylvanus sues to recover from her and her husband Roger Seckerstone certain documents relating to the paternal estate. She was again a widow in 1606. Till a very recent time there were descendants of Spenser living in the south of Ireland.

1869   JOHN W. HALES.
Revised 1896.

Notes

{1} This poem is in this volume reprinted from the edition of 1591. Mr. Morris thinks that Todd was not aware of this edition. Mr. Collier reprinted from the 2nd edition--that of 1593.

{2} ***Irish Minstrelsy; or, Bardic Remains of Ireland***, by J. Hardiman. London, 1831.

{3} 'The name and occupation of Spenser is handed down traditionally among them (the Irish); but they seem to entertain no sentiments of respect or affection for his memory; the bard came in rather ungracious times, and the keen recollections of this untutored people are wonderful.'--Trotter's Walks through Ireland in the Years 1812, 1814, and 1817. London, 1819, p. 302.

{4} Cooper's *Athen. Cantab.*

{5} See Mr. Edwards's *Life of Raleigh*, vol. i. p. 128.

{6} No doubt he intended to complete his work. See book vi. canto v. st. 2:

'When time shall be to tell the same;'

but this time never was.

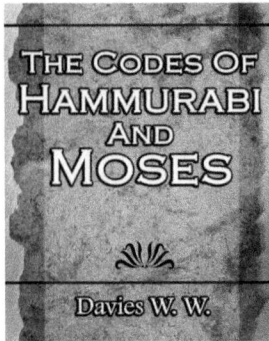

The Codes Of Hammurabi And Moses
W. W. Davies

QTY

The discovery of the Hammurabi Code is one of the greatest achievements of archaeology, and is of paramount interest, not only to the student of the Bible, but also to all those interested in ancient history...

Religion **ISBN:** *1-59462-338-4* **Pages:132**

MSRP $12.95

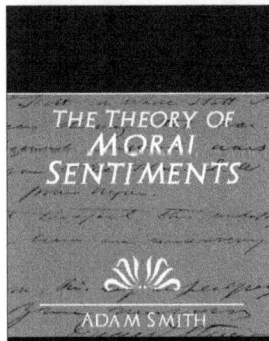

The Theory of Moral Sentiments
Adam Smith

QTY

This work from 1749. contains original theories of conscience amd moral judgment and it is the foundation for systemof morals.

Philosophy **ISBN:** *1-59462-777-0* **Pages:536**

MSRP $19.95

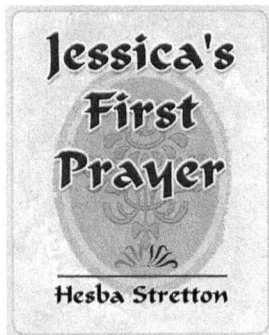

Jessica's First Prayer
Hesba Stretton

QTY

In a screened and secluded corner of one of the many railway-bridges which span the streets of London there could be seen a few years ago, from five o'clock every morning until half past eight, a tidily set-out coffee-stall, consisting of a trestle and board, upon which stood two large tin cans, with a small fire of charcoal burning under each so as to keep the coffee boiling during the early hours of the morning when the work-people were thronging into the city on their way to their daily toil...

Pages:84

Childrens **ISBN:** *1-59462-373-2* *MSRP $9.95*

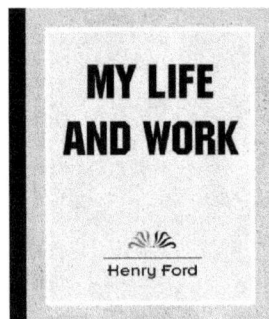

My Life and Work
Henry Ford

QTY

Henry Ford revolutionized the world with his implementation of mass production for the Model T automobile. Gain valuable business insight into his life and work with his own auto-biography... "We have only started on our development of our country we have not as yet, with all our talk of wonderful progress, done more than scratch the surface. The progress has been wonderful enough but..."

Pages:300

Biographies/ **ISBN:** *1-59462-198-5* *MSRP $21.95*

QTY

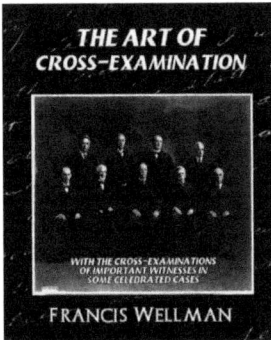

The Art of Cross-Examination
Francis Wellman

I presume it is the experience of every author, after his first book is published upon an important subject, to be almost overwhelmed with a wealth of ideas and illustrations which could readily have been included in his book, and which to his own mind, at least, seem to make a second edition inevitable. Such certainly was the case with me; and when the first edition had reached its sixth impression in five months, I rejoiced to learn that it seemed to my publishers that the book had met with a sufficiently favorable reception to justify a second and considerably enlarged edition. ..

Reference   ISBN: *1-59462-647-2*

Pages:412

MSRP $19.95

QTY

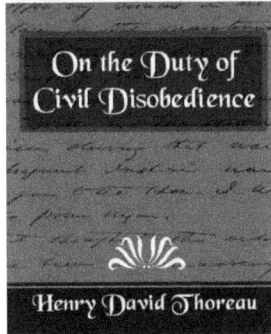

On the Duty of Civil Disobedience
Henry David Thoreau

Thoreau wrote his famous essay, On the Duty of Civil Disobedience, as a protest against an unjust but popular war and the immoral but popular institution of slave-owning. He did more than write—he declined to pay his taxes, and was hauled off to gaol in consequence. Who can say how much this refusal of his hastened the end of the war and of slavery ?

Law   ISBN: *1-59462-747-9*

Pages:48

MSRP $7.45

QTY

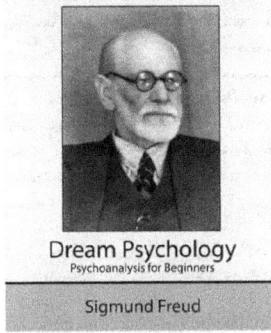

Dream Psychology Psychoanalysis for Beginners
Sigmund Freud

Sigmund Freud, born Sigismund Schlomo Freud (May 6, 1856 - September 23, 1939), was a Jewish-Austrian neurologist and psychiatrist who co-founded the psychoanalytic school of psychology. Freud is best known for his theories of the unconscious mind, especially involving the mechanism of repression; his redefinition of sexual desire as mobile and directed towards a wide variety of objects; and his therapeutic techniques, especially his understanding of transference in the therapeutic relationship and the presumed value of dreams as sources of insight into unconscious desires.

Psychology   ISBN: *1-59462-905-6*

Pages:196

MSRP $15.45

QTY

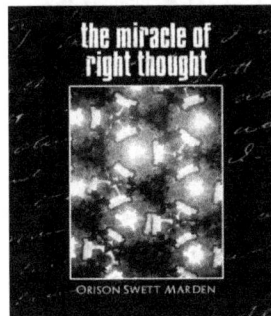

The Miracle of Right Thought
Orison Swett Marden

Believe with all of your heart that you will do what you were made to do. When the mind has once formed the habit of holding cheerful, happy, prosperous pictures, it will not be easy to form the opposite habit. It does not matter how improbable or how far away this realization may see, or how dark the prospects may be, if we visualize them as best we can, as vividly as possible, hold tenaciously to them and vigorously struggle to attain them, they will gradually become actualized, realized in the life. But a desire, a longing without endeavor, a yearning abandoned or held indifferently will vanish without realization.

Self Help   ISBN: *1-59462-644-8*

Pages:360

MSRP $25.45

The Rosicrucian Cosmo-Conception Mystic Christianity *by Max Heindel*   ISBN: *1-59462-188-8*   **$38.95**
The Rosicrucian Cosmo-conception is not dogmatic, neither does it appeal to any other authority than the reason of the student. It is: not controversial, but is: sent forth in the, hope that it may help to clear...   New Age/Religion Pages 646

Abandonment To Divine Providence *by Jean-Pierre de Caussade*   ISBN: *1-59462-228-0*   **$25.95**
"The Rev. Jean Pierre de Caussade was one of the most remarkable spiritual writers of the Society of Jesus in France in the 18th Century. His death took place at Toulouse in 1751. His works have gone through many editions and have been republished...   Inspirational/Religion Pages 400

Mental Chemistry *by Charles Haanel*   ISBN: *1-59462-192-6*   **$23.95**
Mental Chemistry allows the change of material conditions by combining and appropriately utilizing the power of the mind. Much like applied chemistry creates something new and unique out of careful combinations of chemicals the mastery of mental chemistry...   New Age Pages 354

The Letters of Robert Browning and Elizabeth Barret Barrett 1845-1846 vol II   ISBN: *1-59462-193-4*   **$35.95**
by Robert Browning and Elizabeth Barrett   Biographies Pages 596

Gleanings In Genesis (volume I) *by Arthur W. Pink*   ISBN: *1-59462-130-6*   **$27.45**
Appropriately has Genesis been termed "the seed plot of the Bible" for in it we have, in germ form, almost all of the great doctrines which are afterwards fully developed in the books of Scripture which follow...   Religion/Inspirational Pages 420

The Master Key *by L. W. de Laurence*   ISBN: *1-59462-001-6*   **$30.95**
In no branch of human knowledge has there been a more lively increase of the spirit of research during the past few years than in the study of Psychology, Concentration and Mental Discipline. The requests for authentic lessons in Thought Control, Mental Discipline and...   New Age/Business Pages 422

The Lesser Key Of Solomon Goetia *by L. W. de Laurence*   ISBN: *1-59462-092-X*   **$9.95**
This translation of the first book of the "Lernegton" which is now for the first time made accessible to students of Talismanic Magic was done, after careful collation and edition, from numerous Ancient Manuscripts in Hebrew, Latin, and French...   New Age/Occult Pages 92

Rubaiyat Of Omar Khayyam *by Edward Fitzgerald*   ISBN:*1-59462-332-5*   **$13.95**
Edward Fitzgerald, whom the world has already learned, in spite of his own efforts to remain within the shadow of anonymity, to look upon as one of the rarest poets of the century, was born at Bredfield, in Suffolk, on the 31st of March, 1809. He was the third son of John Purcell...   Music Pages 172

Ancient Law *by Henry Maine*   ISBN: *1-59462-128-4*   **$29.95**
The chief object of the following pages is to indicate some of the earliest ideas of mankind, as they are reflected in Ancient Law, and to point out the relation of those ideas to modern thought.   Religiom/History Pages 452

Far-Away Stories *by William J. Locke*   ISBN: *1-59462-129-2*   **$19.45**
"Good wine needs no bush," but a collection of mixed vintages does. And this book is just such a collection. Some of the stories I do not want to remain buried for ever in the museum files of dead magazine-numbers an author's not unpardonable vanity..."   Fiction Pages 272

Life of David Crockett *by David Crockett*   ISBN: *1-59462-250-7*   **$27.45**
"Colonel David Crockett was one of the most remarkable men of the times in which he lived. Born in humble life, but gifted with a strong will, an indomitable courage, and unremitting perseverance...   Biographies/New Age Pages 424

Lip-Reading *by Edward Nitchie*   ISBN: *1-59462-206-X*   **$25.95**
Edward B. Nitchie, founder of the New York School for the Hard of Hearing, now the Nitchie School of Lip-Reading, Inc, wrote "LIP-READING Principles and Practice". The development and perfecting of this meritorious work on lip-reading was an undertaking...   How-to Pages 400

A Handbook of Suggestive Therapeutics, Applied Hypnotism, Psychic Science   ISBN: *1-59462-214-0*   **$24.95**
by Henry Munro   Health/New Age/Health/Self-help Pages 376

A Doll's House: and Two Other Plays *by Henrik Ibsen*   ISBN: *1-59462-112-8*   **$19.95**
Henrik Ibsen created this classic when in revolutionary 1848 Rome. Introducing some striking concepts in playwriting for the realist genre, this play has been studied the world over.   Fiction/Classics/Plays 308

The Light of Asia *by sir Edwin Arnold*   ISBN: *1-59462-204-3*   **$13.95**
In this poetic masterpiece, Edwin Arnold describes the life and teachings of Buddha. The man who was to become known as Buddha to the world was born as Prince Gautama of India but he rejected the worldly riches and abandoned the reigns of power when...   Religion/History/Biographies Pages 170

The Complete Works of Guy de Maupassant *by Guy de Maupassant*   ISBN: *1-59462-157-8*   **$16.95**
"For days and days, nights and nights, I had dreamed of that first kiss which was to consecrate our engagement, and I knew not on what spot I should put my lips..."   Fiction/Classics Pages 240

The Art of Cross-Examination *by Francis L. Wellman*   ISBN: *1-59462-309-0*   **$26.95**
Written by a renowned trial lawyer, Wellman imparts his experience and uses case studies to explain how to use psychology to extract desired information through questioning.   How-to/Science/Reference Pages 408

Answered or Unanswered? *by Louisa Vaughan*   ISBN: *1-59462-248-5*   **$10.95**
Miracles of Faith in China   Religion Pages 112

The Edinburgh Lectures on Mental Science (1909) *by Thomas*   ISBN: *1-59462-008-3*   **$11.95**
This book contains the substance of a course of lectures recently given by the writer in the Queen Street Hail, Edinburgh. Its purpose is to indicate the Natural Principles governing the relation between Mental Action and Material Conditions...   New Age/Psychology Pages 148

Ayesha *by H. Rider Haggard*   ISBN: *1-59462-301-5*   **$24.95**
Verily and indeed it is the unexpected that happens! Probably if there was one person upon the earth from whom the Editor of this, and of a certain previous history, did not expect to hear again...   Classics Pages 380

Ayala's Angel *by Anthony Trollope*   ISBN: *1-59462-352-X*   **$29.95**
The two girls were both pretty, but Lucy who was twenty-one who supposed to be simple and comparatively unattractive, whereas Ayala was credited, as her Bombwhat romantic name might show, with poetic charm and a taste for romance. Ayala when her father died was nineteen...   Fiction Pages 484

The American Commonwealth *by James Bryce*   ISBN: *1-59462-286-8*   **$34.45**
An interpretation of American democratic political theory. It examines political mechanics and society from the perspective of Scotsman James Bryce   Politics Pages 572

Stories of the Pilgrims *by Margaret P. Pumphrey*   ISBN: *1-59462-116-0*   **$17.95**
This book explores pilgrims religious oppression in England as well as their escape to Holland and eventual crossing to America on the Mayflower, and their early days in New England...   History Pages 268

QTY

The Fasting Cure *by Sinclair Upton*   ISBN: *1-59462-222-1* **$13.95**
In the Cosmopolitan Magazine for May, 1910, and in the Contemporary Review (London) for April, 1910, I published an article dealing with my experiences in fasting. I have written a great many magazine articles, but never one which attracted so much attention... New Age/Self Help/Health Pages 164

Hebrew Astrology *by Sepharial*   ISBN: *1-59462-308-2* **$13.45**
In these days of advanced thinking it is a matter of common observation that we have left many of the old landmarks behind and that we are now pressing forward to greater heights and to a wider horizon than that which represented the mind-content of our progenitors... Astrology Pages 144

Thought Vibration or The Law of Attraction in the Thought World   ISBN: *1-59462-127-6* **$12.95**

by William Walker Atkinson   *Psychology/Religion Pages 144*

Optimism *by Helen Keller*   ISBN: *1-59462-108-X* **$15.95**
Helen Keller was blind, deaf, and mute since 19 months old, yet famously learned how to overcome these handicaps, communicate with the world, and spread her lectures promoting optimism. An inspiring read for everyone... Biographies/Inspirational Pages 84

Sara Crewe *by Frances Burnett*   ISBN: *1-59462-360-0*   **$9.45**
In the first place, Miss Minchin lived in London. Her home was a large, dull, tall one, in a large, dull square, where all the houses were alike, and all the sparrows were alike, and where all the door-knockers made the same heavy sound... Childrens/Classic Pages 88

The Autobiography of Benjamin Franklin *by Benjamin Franklin*   ISBN: *1-59462-135-7* **$24.95**
The Autobiography of Benjamin Franklin has probably been more extensively read than any other American historical work, and no other book of its kind has had such ups and downs of fortune. Franklin lived for many years in England, where he was agent... Biographies/History Pages 332

Name	
Email	
Telephone	
Address	
City, State ZIP	

☐ **Credit Card**   ☐ **Check / Money Order**

Credit Card Number	
Expiration Date	
Signature	

Please Mail to: Book Jungle
PO Box 2226
Champaign, IL 61825
or Fax to: 630-214-0564

ORDERING INFORMATION
web*: www.bookjungle.com*
email*: sales@bookjungle.com*
fax*: 630-214-0564*
mail*: Book Jungle PO Box 2226 Champaign, IL 61825*
or PayPal *to sales@bookjungle.com*

Please contact us for bulk discounts

DIRECT-ORDER TERMS

**20% Discount if You Order
Two or More Books**
Free Domestic Shipping!
Accepted: Master Card, Visa,
Discover, American Express

www.ingramcontent.com/pod-product-compliance
Lightning Source LLC
LaVergne TN
LVHW081324060426
835511LV00011B/1845